Reinventing Development Economics

N.A. Mujumdar is a distinguished economist whose PhD thesis from Mumbai University was much acclaimed and published as a book titled: *Some Problems of Underemployment*. He has wide interests in rural issues (particularly the food economy), monetary and fiscal policies, and international issues. He taught at Mumbai University and had the distinction of being awarded the prestigious Nuffield Fellowship at Oxford. On his return to India, he joined the Reserve Bank of India (RBI) in 1960, as research Officer, and retired as Principal Adviser, Department of Economic Analysis and Policy in 1988. He also headed the Monetary Policy Unit of the RBI. His services were sought by the International Monetary Fund (IMF) for secondment to the central banks of five different countries—Zambia, Mauritius, Tanzania, Belize and Cambodia.

After retirement from the RBI, He was Adviser, Central Bank of India, Housing Development Corporation (HDFC), Society for Development Studies (New Delhi) and Adviser on the RBI History Project. Presently, he is Editor of the *Indian Journal of Agricultural Economics*. Dr Mujumdar has been a regular columnist on economic issues since 1988. He has also published eight books. His most recent book on *India's New Development Agenda* was published in 2011 by the Academic Foundation, New Delhi.

Reinventing Development Economics

Explorations from the Indian Experiment

N.A. Mujumdar

ACADEMIC FOUNDATION
NEW DELHI

www.academicfoundation.com

First published in 2014
by

ACADEMIC FOUNDATION
4772-73 / 23 Bharat Ram Road, (23 Ansari Road),
Darya Ganj, New Delhi - 110 002 (India).
Phones : 23245001 / 02 / 03 / 04.
Fax : +91-11-23245005.
E-mail : books@academicfoundation.com
www.academicfoundation.com

Cataloging in Publication Data--DK
Courtesy: D.K. Agencies (P) Ltd. <docinfo@dkagencies.com>

Mujumdar, N. A.
Reinventing development economics : explorations from the Indian experiment / N.A. Mujumdar.
p. cm.
ISBN 9789332701250

1. Economic development--India. 2. Monetary policy--India.
3. India--Economic policy--1991- I. Title.

DDC 330.954 23

Typeset by Italics India, New Delhi.

Printed and bound by The Book Mint, New Delhi.
www.thebookmint.in

To My Father Annaji

Contents

II
Monetary Policy

III
Banking Policy

IV
Fiscal Policy

V
Food Security

VI
Global Environment

Introduction

DEVELOPMENT economics is now a failed God. This is true both in terms of theoretical constructs and policy inputs. Attempts by economists like Robert Solow to capture the essentials of growth in a mathematical or econometric formula were, it appears in retrospect, misdirected. The World Bank (WB) sponsored Commission on Growth and Development asserts that there is no generic formula for growth (2008). "Each Country has specific characteristics and historical experiences that must be reflected in its growth story". Secondly, a recent critical appraisal of the much-touted WB's *World Development Reports* (WDRs) has revealed that these were empty vessels offering little meaningful development policy guidelines. In a seminal paper published recently the WB has frankly confessed the infirmities of development economics and has written, as it were, a virtual obituary of development economics (April 2012).

The dimensions of development have also taken a new shape. As Recupero Rubans puts it: "We should never forget the economy is not something that is beyond our control. The market has to be our servant, not our master. The economy is not like the planetary system or the genetic code: something that is given once and for all and which one cannot alter: it is a product of culture, it is a product of human choices: of choice of values. That is why we have to choose the right value and put competition exactly in balance with other values and decide what are the higher values for us. We have particularly to provide people with tangible reasons to hope for the future". This takes us well beyond growth models to the realm of philosophy of development. We must grow up from the conventional growth economics trapped in market theology to resonate to the larger concerns of holistic development including promotion of broad-based, decentralised growth which alone could facilitate access by the poor to employment, food, nutrition and health, and quality education.

Moreover, it has now been recognised that inclusive growth is imperative for sustainability. To quote Dr. Subbarao, Governor, Reserve Bank of India: "Over the past 60 years, we have seen several episodes of economic growth in different parts of the world. One clear lesson of this experience is that growth is sustainable only if it is inclusive. Governments around the world are therefore anxious that even as they pursue economic growth they must make that growth process inclusive." This strong linkage between stability and inclusion should be the guiding principle of our policies for promotion of growth. In this context, putting in place appropriate safety nets to reduce the vulnerability of the poor, and above all to build a value-based compassionate society assume added significance. Provision of a basic "social protection floor" thus becomes an ineluctable necessity.

In fact the crash of American capitalism in the 2010s has brought into sharp focus the new dimension of development economics. The collapse of the American capitalistic model in 2002 and the global financial crisis of 2008 reflected in all its rawness the workings of predatory capitalism. The Financial Inquiry Commission has laid bare for all to see the shameless greed and moral decadness of the Wall Street banker. The 'Occupy Wall Street Movement' reflects the public resentment over the behaviour of financial actors. Nearer home, Rajat Gupta's case is a concrete example of selling one's soul for mess of pottage.

There is now a call for revival of ethical values. The American Economic Association has mooted the idea of Code of Ethics for finance professionals, regulators and academics. Robert Shiller proposes that "the best way to do this is to build good moral behaviour into the culture of Wall Street..." In certain advanced countries there is disenchantment with 'casino banking culture' and erosion of trust in the financial sector as a whole. To restore the trust, Dr. Reddy, former Governor of Reserve Bank of India, has advocated 'inclusive finance'—a commitment to access of essential financial services to all segments of the society.

"Society has put its trust in Central Banks. Central Banks have to ensure that bank managements and financial sector in general serve the masses and not merely the elite or financially active. In the ultimate analysis, Central banks are trustees, agents to look after the interest of masses."

Some countries like India were not affected directly by the global financial meltdown of 2008. But the adverse impact of 'external shock'—external in the sense of external to domestic economy—on poverty cannot be ignored. For instance, the sharp rise in world food prices played havoc with the poor. The Food and Agriculture Organization (FAO) index of real food prices began rising in 2002 and spiked sharply in 2006 and 2007. By mid-2008 real food prices were 64 per cent higher than their level in 2002. FAO estimates that mainly as a result of high food prices, the number of chronically hunger people in the world rose by 75 million in 2007. The devastating effect of high food prices on the number of hungry people is thus clear. Similarly, the global financial crisis 2008, according to UN estimates, resulted in the addition of some 47 million to the pool of extreme poverty. Crises of this nature set the clock of eliminating hunger back. How do we protect the vulnerable sections of the population during phases of such external shocks?

If we need to rewrite the script of development economics, how do we go about it? India's development experience during the two decades 1991-2011 provides good insights into the issue moving away from Milton Friedman towards Mahatma Gandhi, away from market theology towards building a value-based society. Deriving lessons from this empirical experience, this bunch of 54 articles collected in this book seeks to reconstruct the new philosophy of economic development. The book is thus an attempt at exploring the new dimensions of development philosophy. Some episodes of global experience during this phase also form part of this exploratory exercise.

The book is divided into six broad sections: Growth and Development, Monetary Policy, Banking Policy, Fiscal Policy, Food Security and Global Environment. Each article is intrinsically important for the subject it deals with. But all of them are anchored in the underlying main theme of promoting growth which is all-round and inclusive, equitable and above all growth which ultimately leads to the emergence of value-based compassionate society.

Recently, there was in India public outrage against rampant corruption which manifested itself in the Anna Hazare movement. Again, the epidemic of rape has resulted in the public outrage nationwide. But these are symptoms of a sick society. If improvement in the quality of life is the end objective of all development endeavours, the need to tackle such sickness becomes imperative.

Indian philosophy offers a remedy. It advocates the need to build 'development conscience' among all sections of the population. From times immemorial, Indian philosophy has maintained that all-round development of the society is best achieved through betterment of the individual which includes economic well-being but extends well beyond it. Social conscience must be inculcated among individuals through education at all stages and also professional training. All individuals must be sensitised in their young age itself to the abject poverty, the squalor, disease, ignorance and illiteracy that surround us. They must be made to begin to think in terms of what is our *dharma* or duty towards alleviating some of the infirmities that affect our less fortunate fellow human beings.

One of the ancient scriptures of India, *Brahadaranyaka Upanishad* enjoins that our life must be guided by the following three "*Das*". *Damyata*, that is control yourself; *Datta* that is give to others; and *Dayadhwam*, that is be compassionate. Thus we must practice self-control, charity, and be compassionate. The *Bhagawad Gita* enjoins us to treat others as you treat yourself (*atmanpamyena*). What is good for you is good for others; what is bad for you is bad for others. Learn to rejoice in doing good to all creatures. Inculcating these qualities among individuals will go a long way towards eliminating society's sicknesses like corruption, improving the quality of life and in general evolving a caring and compassionate society.

Most of the articles included in this book were published in the *Free Press Journal* as my fortnightly column. My grateful thanks to Shri Jagdish Rattanani, Business Editor, *Free Press Journal*, for permitting me to bring them out in a book form. My thanks are also due to Ms Vijaya Venkatesh for research assistance and Ms Anita Shetty for secretarial assistance.

My association with the Academic Foundation goes back to 2002 when they published my book: *Financial Sector Reforms and India's Economic Development*. Dr (Mrs) Uma Kapila has always taken a personal interest in the publication of my books and I am indeed grateful to her. My thanks are also due to her colleagues in the Academic Foundation for expeditious publication of the book.

—N.A. Mujumdar

I

Growth and Development

1

India's Development Drama (1991-2011)

From Milton Friedman to Mahatma Gandhi

Introduction

Admittedly, India's growth story is impressive with GDP growth recording an annual average growth of 8.5 per cent during the five years—2003 to 2008. Even during the year 2009-10 of global meltdown, India managed to post a growth of 7.2 per cent. In the medium term, it is reasonable to expect the economy to resume its robust growth path of around 9 per cent. This is indeed beyond all expectations for an economy which was supposed to be condemned to a Hindu rate of growth of 3 per cent.

In the euphoria of sustained high growth, we generally tend to overlook the mistakes committed by our policy-makers during this period of liberalisation. The period of the so-called economic reforms—a period of liberalisation of the Indian economy from 1991 to 2004—I would submit, was the most retrogressive phase in the history of India's economic development. We may not have our own Reagonomics or Thatcherism to bury but our policy-makers during this period were soaked in the market theology of the International Monetary Fund (IMF)/World Bank. The focus was on liberalisation, market-led growth, fiscal correction, promotion of private and foreign investment, development of the capital market, and generally creating of an environment of consumerism. More basic issues of development were overlooked which led to neglect of agriculture, disdain for subsidies, whether food subsidy or credit subsidy, and more disturbingly disregard for the elementary principles of food security.

A word about the theme of my paper.[1] I have chosen to focus on India's economic development during the last two decades i.e., 1991-2011 with a purpose. I have divided the period into two distinct phases: the first from 1991-2004, a period of liberalisation and economic reforms, which I have called the Milton Friedman phase. Intoxicated with the philosophy of market-led growth of the IMF/World Bank, our policy-makers went about ruthlessly seeking higher growth rate, with all its adverse effects on development issues. The second phase (2004-2011), which I have called the Mahatma Gandhi phase, is a period when Indian policy-makers began to rediscover, as it were, Mahatma Gandhi's development philosophy. Community-centred development holds the key to policy pursued during this phase, when policy-makers are even dreaming of a sort of food utopia. The second phase represents a dramatic departure from the policies pursued in the first phase. Thus, there is an element of drama in our approach to development. This dramatic change has to be judged against the global financial and economic crisis of 2008 which has dramatically changed the institutional and policy-making landscape. This crisis in a way reflected the loss of faith in the capitalist system led by unbridled market forces. This takes us well beyond growth models to the realm of economic philosophy of development. We must grow up from the conventional growth models trapped in the market theology to resonate to the larger concerns of holistic development including promotion of broad-based decentralised growth which alone could facilitate access by the poor to employment, food, nutrition and health, and quality education and to putting in place safety nets to reduce the vulnerability of the poor. The proposed Food Security Act reflects the crux of new agenda of development. If the conventional development economics is a failed God, are we now re-writing the script of development economics? We have to judge the Indian

1. This theme and sub-themes have been developed over the years. For any further documentation and evidence in support of the statements made here, the reader is invited to refer to my following books. *Financial Sector Reforms and India's Economic Development*, two volumes (2002); *Economic Reforms Sans Development* (2004); *Inclusive Growth: Development Perspectives in Indian Economy* (2007); *India's New Development Agenda: Building a Value-based Society* (2011). All these books are published by Academic Foundation, New Delhi.

development experience in the broader context of disillusionment with development economics as a discipline. The frontiers of development economics are expanding further. The 'commitment deficit' of our policy-makers and development administration, as we will spell out shortly, is impairing the outcome of our development efforts. The recent mass outbursts against widespread corruption raise another related issue of national character. Do these developments reinforce the imperative need to build a value-based and compassionate society? We should ponder over.

Milton Friedman Phase: 1991-2004

During this phase, the growth culture itself seems to have gone through a fundamental change with reformers repeating parrot-like phrases borrowed from the IMF/World Bank vocabulary: 'There is no free lunch,' perhaps meaning that the poor must fend for themselves. Despite graduating to the league of fast growing economies of the world, India continues to be the abode of the largest number of underfed and undernourished people in the world. The Food and Agriculture Organization (FAO) estimates show that the number of undernourished people in India has risen from 206 million in 1990-1992 to 230.5 million in 2003-2005, a rise of some 24 million. The Human Development Index (HDI) of the United Nation Development Programme (UNDP) (2009) ranks India as the 134th out of 182 countries of the world. The HDI is based on three indicators, namely, GDP per capita, life expectancy at birth, and education as measured by adult literacy rate and gross enrollment ratio. India is thus still in the Medium Human Development category with even countries like China, Sri Lanka and Indonesia having higher ranking.

A community-centred analysis thus exposes clearly the darker side of the development policy pursued during this period. While there is enough literature on the harm inflicted on the economy by the centrally planned economic phase—the so-called Licence Permit *Raj*—little attention has been paid to the negative impact of the pursuit of unbridled market theology during the 1991-2004 phase. Economic historians need to pay greater attention to this aspect.

What is ironical was that this approach to development came to be adopted at a period when the American capitalist model collapsed in 2008. Market fundamentalism embodied in the neoliberalism based on the notion that markets are self-correcting, allocate resources efficiently and serve the public interest well has collapsed. The so-called 'Washington Consensus' in favour of privatisation and liberalisation now stands stripped of its sanctimonious robe. It has now become clear that unbridled market forces are not self-correcting, regulation and direction of some sort is needed. This state has a critical role to play in the management of the economy.

I would be content with citing the following five concrete instances to substantiate how the mindless pursuit of market theology during the phase de-emphasised development: food grains management, watershed development as part of the broader theme: home-grown green revolution, inequitable interest rate structure, the microfinance mess and fiscal inequity. At some point of time in the economic history of a nation, there arise occasions when somebody has to speak the truth like the innocent boy who spoke out about the emperor's clothes. As one who is engaged in the study of India's economic development for the last five decades, and now with one foot in the grave, as it were, I thought I am qualified to do the job and hence I have set out to do it not so much in anger as in agony, agony because Indian economic development has some elements of a Greek tragedy as illustrated with some episodes.

India is a pioneer in development planning having launched its First Five Year Plan in 1951. After six decades of development planning, alas, we are still pre-occupied with measuring poverty. Three officially sponsored reports proposing new method for identification of the poor and for the measurement and eradication of poverty have been brought out in 2009. Dr Shylendra who has done an excellent critical review of these reports comes to the conclusion that, "we are no wiser than before about poverty and ways of tackling it" (Shylendra, 2010). He asserts that under the current political economy "there seems to be no escape from the prevailing muddle over understanding poverty and the trap of reformism laid by the neoliberal framework in our efforts to banish poverty." What a travesty of development planning.

Reverting to development, Avinash Dixit asks: "what feature or features of policies are important for good economic outcomes regard-less of what kind of government makes those policies? Here much of the literature does find one point of agreement: credibility of commitments is vital" (Dixit, 2006). During this phase of India's development, it is the commitment deficit which stands out as a villain of the tragedy.

Let us now take up the five concrete cases.

Food Grains Management Policy

The most disturbing policy during this phase was that India chose to export a huge quantity of 27 million tonnes of rice and wheat during the three consecutive years 2001-02 to 2003-04. This was the result of two regressive measures taken earlier; first, the Government introduced in 1997 targeting the public distribution system (PDS) in the form of targeted public distribution system (TPDS). This narrow targeting of the PDS based on absolute income poverty excluded a large part of the nutritionally vulnerable population from PDS due to the continuous raising of the issue price of food grains—inspired by the objective of cutting the size of food subsidies. The concessionally priced food grains became increasingly inaccessible to the poor. The inevitable consequence was the mounting food stocks with the Food Corporation of India (FCI). At one time, the stocks reached a peak of 60 million tonnes. No wonder our policy-makers sought the soft option in exports for tackling the so-called 'surplus food grains' problem. This was nothing short of development atrocity when viewed against the background of India being the abode of the largest number of underfed and undernourished persons in the world, as mentioned earlier.

The irony was compounded further: while the policy-makers' ostensible objective was to reduce subsidies for domestic consumption of food grains, the same policy-makers did not have any qualms about subsidising exports of food grains. If Mahatma Gandhi were alive perhaps, one could speculate there would have been a satyagraha against such mindless pursuit of flawed food grains management policy.

Bhikhu Parekh has admirably encapsulated the poverty profile, as sketched by the Mahatma, in the following paragraph:

> ...Second, poverty dehumanises human beings, wastes the potential and deprives their lives of all sense of meaning and purpose. It is one of the worst violence that human beings can commit against other human beings. It is as bad as killing, and even worse for the fact that it is silent, slow and invisible, arouses no anger and is outside the purview of anyone's direct responsibility. As long as even one person is starved, is malnourished or lacks decent housing, the social order stands indicted lacking legitimacy. Basic human needs have the first claim on Society's resources, and it is an obligation to arrange its economic affairs in a manner that the needs of all members are met. (Sharma, 2007)

In my Introduction to a book on agriculture, I wrote in 2006:

> It was tragic enough for a predominantly agricultural economy not to be able to produce in the 1960s adequate quantities of food grains to meet the domestic consumption requirements of the population: it is perhaps a greater systemic tragedy today that even when we are able to produce adequate quantities of food grains we are unable to ensure that food grains so produced do reach the needy. (Mujumdar and Kapila, 2007)

Hunger and poverty are an affront to a civilised society and subsidies are a characteristic of a civilised society. One begins to wonder whether we are dismissing poverty or reduction of poverty as mere phrases of a dialectic process, denying thereby its moral urgency of addressing the task.

Ironically, the pendulum seems to have swung to the other extreme. Today, the National Food Security Bill, 2011, seeks to create a sort of 'food utopia' by seeking to ensure 'home delivery,' as it were, of a specified quantum, of subsidised food grains to the bulk of the population. We will discuss it presently.

Home-grown Green Revolution: Watershed Development

It has become fashionable to harp on the theme that a second green revolution can alone ensure food security in the current scenario. The first green revolution was achieved through a genetic breakthrough in seed technology, a technology which was accessible to all. Today the circumstances are different. I would submit there are more mundane and less glamorous alternatives to attain food and nutrition security, perhaps not wholly but substantially. One does not have to 'import' farm technology, as we did in 1960s.

Future agricultural growth will have to be necessarily water-centric and what better alternative there could be than watershed development, which I regard as the mother of all water management modes. Watershed development projects, both micro and macro, hold out great promise for future agricultural growth; the potential area to be covered is huge, with about 60 per cent of the area under crops being rainfed; capital investment is modest, the projects are labour intensive and do not require much technical know-how. By its very nature, growth under watershed development is 'inclusive.'

Yet, why despite all the sound and fury, we have not made any appreciable progress? For instance, the Macro Management of Agriculture (MMA) assistance during 2010-11 has been used to treat a mere 3 lakh ha of land under the National Water Development Programme for Rainfed Areas (NWDPRA).

In fact watershed development programmes have a fairly long history. It was in 1986 that the NWDPRA was introduced in 99 districts in 16 states. But, what has happened in the subsequent quarter century? The Government of India (GoI) issued in 2008 'The Common Guidelines for Watershed Development Projects'—the first set of guidelines that apply to watershed development projects across three GoI ministries—Ministry of Rural Development, Ministry of Agriculture and Ministry of Environment and Forests. Trust the bureaucracy of mystify, sometimes with a little help from academicians, a perfectly simple and workable growth tool. We have had scholarly discourses on watershed development like the Parthasarathy Committee Report. There is enough of sound and fury. But where are the results? Even in a progressive state like Maharashtra, the proportion of area covered by micro watershed development to the total eligible area is not significant.

It is necessary to demystify the whole approach to watershed development. Considering the humble animal—watershed development—the punditry and complexity of the 'Guidelines' mentioned above is astounding. In contrast, look at the success stories of individual initiatives. In Maharashtra, Anna Hazare's Ralegan Siddhi project has now become a part of folklore of watershed movement. A more recent case is that of Hiware Bazar, a drought-prone poverty-stricken village about 100 km from Pune. The efforts of one man Popatrao Baguji Pawar have converted this village into a model village (*adarsh gaon*). The International Groundwater Association has given to this village the International Groundwater Management Award. Neither Hazare nor Pawar could have read and appreciated the erudition and comprehensiveness of the 'Guidelines,' referred to above. Yet they were able to evolve their own region and location-specific models and emerge as the new Schumpeterian heroes of agricultural growth and rural development. There may be similar leaders in Gujarat, Rajasthan and elsewhere. It may be useful to produce the growth profiles of these successful stories so that we may be able to replicate them, on a large scale.

The mid-term appraisals of Plans of relevant states should have contained a separate section on the progress of watershed development projects. Alas! This is not so. All this shows a sort of 'commitment deficit' on the part of policy-makers and the development administration.

Take another instance of our policy-makers' high profile initiatives—the India-US collaboration on agricultural technology. The 'Joint Statement of Prime Minister Manmohan Singh and President Barack Obama' issued on November 8, 2010, at the end of the latter's visit to India mentions the decision "to work together to develop, test, and replicate transformative technologies to extend food security, as part of the Evergreen Revolution.' The Prime Minister has lauded the US's role in launching India's first green revolution, transforming Indian agricultural production and has welcomed US collaboration in spurring a 'second green revolution' (see *Economic and Political Weekly*, December 11, 2010). We must remember that much of the inventions of high-yielding varieties of seeds that launched India's first green revolution took place under the auspices of publicly funded research institutions. But today the intellectual property rights (IPR) of the genetically modified (GM) seeds are held by the Monsantos, DuPonts and Dows. These are purely agribusiness corporations aiming at maximising their profits. They are not freely accessible to all farmers.

One does not have to look to the US to increase the level of yields of our crops even at the current level of technology and farm management practices. The gap between the yields in our agriculture research centres at the state level and the actual farm level is quite wide: for example, in the case of wheat it is 84 per cent for Madhya Pradesh; for rice over 100 per cent in Assam, Bihar, Chhattisgarh and Uttar Pradesh; for soyabean 185 per cent in Karnataka; and for sugarcane it is 167 per cent in Madhya Pradesh. Hence, if we can bridge these yield gaps, we can increase production by 50 per cent. Over the years, unfortunately, we have de-emphasised the role of agricultural extension services—which played a critical role in facilitating the first green revolution and today the services have become practically dysfunctional. Of course, we must rejuvenate these services. Given the poor state of government extension services, we could induce public sector banks (PSBs) to extend their help. In the past, performance of PSBs in this area was excellent. We may renew such efforts (Khan, 2010).

We could have a time-bound programme of development of watershed projects, covering the bulk of the eligible area in the country in the next two or three years. Perhaps the Mahatma Gandhi National Rural Employment Guarantee Scheme (MGNREGS) could in the relevant regions be made to focus on these projects. Such concerted action pursued with dogged determination could yield good results.

Inequitable Interest Rate Regime

Those who pontificate on why the concessional lending rates do not help the poor further expose their innocence of the realities of the present interest rate structure. Financial sector and banking sector reforms implemented in the 1990s resulted in the emergence of an inequitable interest rate structure, a structure designed to pamper the private corporate sector, and which is biased against agricultural and the small borrower generally. For instance, a small farmer was made to pay an interest rate of 12 per cent at a time when highly rated corporate entity could raise money from banks at 6 per cent. This paradoxical situation was the result of mindless implementation of Basel norms and adoption without adaptation of concepts like 'risks' as understood in the developed world. As I have discussed elsewhere, this concept of 'risks' should be made to stand on its head (Mujumdar, 2005). When some of us raised this question of inequitable interest rate structure in the early 1990s, the Reserve Bank of India (RBI) ignored the protest. Wisdom finally dawned on the RBI in 2005-06 when its *Report on Currency and Finance 2005-06* provided valuable insights into the structure of interest rates. The bulk of bank lending has been taking place at sub-benchmark prime lending rate (sub-BPLR). For instance, the share of sub-BPLR lending increased to 82 per cent by March 2007. While higher credit rated corporates are getting credit at sub-BPLR rates, agriculture and small industry and other small borrowers are generally charged BPLR, or in some cases, above BPLR rates. To quote the RBI report: "to compensate for such sub-BPLR lending, other segments are charged higher rates of interest, thus leading to cross subsidisation of the economically well-off borrowers by the economically poor borrowers" (RBI, 2007). This is indeed disturbing especially when the objective of both the inclusive growth in the real sector as envisaged in the Eleventh Plan and financial inclusion is to promote growth with equity. Although this inequitable situation was modified to some extent by the Government providing interest rate subvention since 2008-09 to ensure that farmers get short-term crop loan upto ₹ 3 lakh at 7 per cent, the basic issue remains. Interestingly enough, none of the reformers of financial sector has identified the problem. It is to the credit to RBI that they brought out the problem in the open and appointed a working group in April 2008 to look into the issue.

The Working Group on Benchmark Prime Lending Rate submitted its report on October 2009. As a result of the Group's recommendation, the banking system switched over from BPLR to the base rate system with effect from July 1, 2010. The base rates set by major banks are in the range of 7.25 per cent to 8 per cent. In retrospect, we can see how the previous interest rate regime 'exploited' the small borrowers, including small farmers, by changing, say, 12 per cent. While the corporate sector is quite vocal in seeking a low interest rate regime for itself on the pretext that high interests would adversely affect growth, our policy-makers were insensitive to the unmerited interest rate burden inflicted on the silent small borrowers. It took two decades for the RBI to correct the distortion in the interest rate structure.

The Microfinance Mess

The recent crisis witnessed by the microfinance sector provides yet another concrete evidence of how RBI has become insensitive to the problems of the small borrower. It seems RBI has yet to recover from the hangover of the market-obsessed reform phobia. I have provided an in-depth analyses of these developments elsewhere (Mujumdar and Shirahatti, 2011) and here I will be content with highlighting the main issues. It is not a case of RBI's benign neglect. RBI became a co-conspirator in the metamorphosis of microfinance institutions (MFIs) into glorified moneylenders charging usurious interest rates of 30-40 per cent. RBI's blessings came in the form of public sector support to the sector. Such support was extended from PSBs, National Bank for Agriculture and Rural Development (NABARD) and Small Industries Development Bank of India (SIDBI). Even after the crisis, RBI's Malegam Committee has 'sanctified' a 26 per cent interest rate for MFIs. This is most unfortunate because historically RBI has the image of a guardian-angel of small farmers or small borrowers generally.

More recent revelations of for-profit MFIs have exposed how these institutions are exploiting the situation in the name of financial inclusion. In addition to the usurious lending rates of 30-40 per cent, the managing directors of some of the biggest MFIs were paid obscenely high remuneration packages of say ₹ 4 crore to ₹ 8 crore—the level higher than that of managing director of HDFC Bank. There was also no transparency in the mutual benefit trusts (MBTs)—shareholding vehicle for MFIs (*Economic Times* investigations). Perhaps, the last nail in the coffin of these for-profit MFIs was hit by the recent statement of Dr Y.V. Reddy, former Governor, RBI, that for-profit MFIs were worse than moneylenders. Moneylender lends out of his own money, whereas MFIs were actually borrowing money from depositors and banks and on-lending the money. So, "MFI is essentially a leveraged moneylender" (*Economic Times*, November 23, 2010). He went on further to add that many finance experts believed, but did not have the courage to admit publicly, that microfinance is India's subprime: "ultimately, it is something like subprime lending." The studied silence of experts has cost the economy a great deal. In retrospect, the Government of Andhra Pradesh deserves to be congratulated on its ordinance issued in 2010 which spelt out clearly the malpractices of such MFIs: "whereas these SHGs are being exploited by private Micro Finance Institutions (MFIs) through usurious interest rates and coercive means of recovery resulting in their impoverishment and in some cases leading to suicides...." This triggered a crisis which almost paralysed for-profit MFIs, with banks reluctant to lend, 'repayments dwindling and depositors tending to withdraw their money.' It is this shock therapy which led to subsequent soul-searching on the part of those MFIs, the promoters of which were fattening themselves on the sweat of the poor borrowers. The microfinance institutions network (MFIN), a grouping of for-profit microlenders, has now set up a committee to look into these deficiencies. In fact, the clout of these MFI seems to be so strong that in spite of all that has been now exposed, some influential papers plead: 'don't kill microfinance.' The short answer to such pleas is: 'we do not want to kill these MFIs; but we certainly want to prevent them from killing their poor borrowers.'

No doubt, the for-profit MFIs represent the predatory face of financial capitalism. But this was compounded by the institutional support which was extended to these MFIs. Such support came from RBI, PSBs, NABARD and SIDBI. For instance, during 2008-09, banks extended loans worth ₹ 3,700 crore. Now, why should PSBs extend loans to MFIs at something like 12 per cent, when they were fully aware that these funds would be on-lend by MFIs at 25-30 per cent? The answer is that such loans by PSBs to MFIs were treated as priority sector lending. So this had the blessings of RBI. Similarly, some equity or quasi-equity support came from SIDBI and NABARD, of course, at concessional rates. RBI could have stipulated that PSBs should lend only to 'not-for-profit category' of MFIs. PSBs could have also stipulated, on their part, that the on-lending rate of beneficiary MFIs should not 'exceed say 17-18 per cent.' This was not done. This systemic support perhaps also lent some respectability to for-profit MFIs. Thus, public sector financial resources were used to perpetuate usurious lending practices of MFIs.

In all humility, we may ask Dr Reddy: it is one thing to say that RBI had no statutory powers to regulate MFIs, but was it obliged to support for-profit MFIs? RBI could have stipulated that PSBs should lend only to not-for-profit MFIs, fixing a ceiling on their on-lending rates. This support made the system, in a manner of speaking, a co-conspirator in this business of exploiting poor rural borrowers. Public funds were allowed to generate private profits. RBI has not covered itself in glory in this episode.

The sordid story does not end here. Because of high returns, some may even say, with obscenely high returns, stemming from exorbitant lending rates, for-profit MFIs have become attractive investment destinations for private equity and venture capitalists. The recent success of initial public offering (IPO) of SKS Microfinance Ltd. is a case in point. It attracted high profile investors like billionaire George Soros, venture capitalist Vinod Khosla and Infosys Founder Narayana Murthy. Alluding to this transformation of the humble animal microfinance, Muhammad Yunus, the father of microfinance movement, said: "it is a complete detour and nothing but a quitting of microfinance mission." The original microfinance concept of helping the poor via small loans at reasonable rates of interest has been abdicated (*Economic Times*, December 13, 2010). Is it a case of Shylocks masquerading as microfinance institutions? One wonders.

Basically, lending to the rural poor at 30-40 per cent defies all economic logic. Our small rural borrowers are not Schumpeterian mini-heroes, who can make the project or activity for financing what they have borrowed financially viable. In fact, by inflating interest cost, we are building *ab initio* non-viability into the project. Secondly, the engagement of for-profit MFIs with borrowers has been shallow based on 'touch and move' business models shorn of any development content. "The average loans per client in both MFIs and SHGs have been low, between ₹ 3500 and ₹ 5000. The duration of the loan is short, typically one year or less. The small loan and the short duration do not enable most borrowers to do much except to ease liquidity problems" (*Microfinance India: State of the Sector Report*, 2008). It was M.L. Darling who wrote long ago that the Indian peasant is born in debt, lives in debt and dies in debt, thanks to the moneylender. Are we trying to promote the Darling syndrome?

It should be underlined that the policy-makers' indifference to exorbitant rural lending rates is in sharp contrast to their concern for corporate sector. Whenever RBI even contemplates raising of repo rates by say 0.25 per cent, the corporate lobby is up in arms, 'don't raise lending rates, it will hurt growth.' More often than not, RBI yields to the corporate sector plea.

Whatever RBI's Malegam Committee has recommended, covers some ground towards reforming the for-profit MFIs. But it seems to have missed the central point. The public sector support to for-profit MFIs should be withdrawn forthwith. After all, why did PSBs begin to extend their support to such MFIs? Because these MFIs provided 'an easy escape route' to their responsibility regarding meeting the priority sector credit target of 40 per cent. In doing so, we have landed ourselves into a greater mess. Then there was this façade of financial inclusion. This empirical experience has demonstrated that under such circumstances, it is better not to have borrowed at all, at prohibitive costs, than borrowed and lost. It is better to remain 'excluded' than 'included.'

Where do we go from here? Indian policy-makers must be reminded that India, unlike many other countries like Bangladesh, for example, has a healthy home-grown segment of microfinance. PSBs, restructured regional rural banks (RRBs) rejuvenated cooperative credit system, NABARD's self-help groups (SHGs)-bank linkage programme (SBLP), which has emerged as a major channel of microfinance. Then there is the post office, which is already functioning as a semi-bank, with its 1.55 lakh branches and some 16 crore customers. This has great potential, given appropriate policy support, to emerge as a low-cost microfinance channel. The point is that these public or semi-public sector segments have successfully blended profitability criteria with social banking. Of course, 'not-for-profit' MFIs are indeed welcome to join the stream. Our policy- makers could do well to refocus their energies on further developing this segment, rather than trying to reform rogue MFIs. In the business of financial inclusion, there is enough pace for not-for-profit MFIs but not for rogue MFIs.

Fiscal Inequity

The Indian fiscal system is distinguished by the fact that dividends received by individuals are totally exempt from income tax without any limit. Similarly, there are exemptions without limit, from long-term capital gains from the stock market. Thus persons receiving thousands of crores of rupees of dividend income are totally free from income tax, while those earning modest incomes from professions are taxed at high rates. These exemptions are sought to justified on the ground that they foster the development of equity market. The ostensible rationale is that since corporate have already paid the tax, taxing dividend income of individuals would be tantamount to double taxation. This is a specious argument. In the idiom of public finance, corporate and individuals are distinct entities and hence they ought to be taxed separately. Dr S.S. Tarapore, former Deputy Governor of RBI, has correctly argued that unlimited exemptions of dividend income are incongruous with distributive justice and are nothing short of fiscal atrocity.

Contrast this with the recent proposition by Warren Buffett, the billionaire investor and founder of Berkshire Hathaway, that the richest should be taxed heavily: 'tax us more.' Supporting this move, France's 16 richest persons have pressed for more taxes. Where are our pretensions to the socialistic pattern of society?

Development Economics: The God that Failed

Before we move on to the discussion of the next stage of India's economic development: 2004-2011, it may be useful to raise some broader questions. Has the process of disillusionment with development economics already started? Let us take a quick look at the more recent developments.

The Commission on Growth and Development sponsored by among others the World Bank submitted its report in June 2008 (World Bank, 2008). The Commission's main recommendations stem from investigations into the empirical experiences of 13 countries, which recorded an average annual gross domestic product (GDP) growth of 7 per cent for 25 years or longer, since 1950. These countries were Botswana, Brazil, China, Hong Kong, Indonesia, Japan, the Republic of Korea, Malaysia, Malta, Oman, Singapore, Taiwan and Thailand. The Commission adds that two other countries—India and Vietnam—were on their way to joining this group.

These success stories demonstrate that fast and sustained growth is possible. At this pace of expansion, an economy almost doubles its size every decade. The Commission rejects the view that these are 'economic miracles.' The Commission believes that there are perfectly rational explanations for these success stories. Distilling the empirical experience of these 13 countries, the Commission comes up with five essential ingredients for faster and sustained growth: (i) these countries fully exploited the world economy; (ii) they maintained macroeconomic stability; (iii) they mustered high rates of saving and investment; (iv) they let markets allocate resources; and (v) they had committed, credible and capable governments.

So far so good. Can these ingredients help us to draw up blue prints for growth and development of other poor countries? "But it is hard to know how to replicate these characteristics," the report reveals.

This is the tragedy of development economics. The Commission admits that there is no generic formula for growth: "Each country has specific characteristics and historical experiences that must be reflected in its growth story." Indian policy-makers in the post-1990s phase were, as we have seen, soaked in the market theology of the IMF and the World Bank and tried to mimic the American capitalist model. This was reflected more prominently in financial sector reforms and in their obsession with privatisation. The Commission itself is cautious that "governments in these high growth economies were not free market 'purists'." We have thus come a long way from conventional development models.

At this stage, it may be appropriate to recall the famous observation of the Nobel Laureate Robert Solow: how often all the discussions of the sources of growth and development seem to end in a blaze of sociology, which also explains the stubbornly large residuals in all growth accounting models. He used his theoretical progress. 'The technological change residual' is so-called because it is part of the growth that cannot be explained by identifiable factors such as capital accumulation or labour force growth. We have today moved well beyond Solow: the five essential ingredients of the growth receipe identified by the Growth Commission demonstrate that it is inappropriate to call other factors—other than the conventional factors like saving rate, capital-output ratio and the rate of growth of labour force—as 'residual.' Bereft of these five elements, growth accounting models, would be reduced to barren econometric exercises. That is how perhaps development economics failed many countries. Our basic approach to development was perhaps flawed.

The disillusionment with development economics was not only in terms of theoretical constructs but also with development policy. When Robert McNamara launched a crusade for poverty eradication as the main goal of the World Bank, the World Bank began to articulate its development vision through its *World Development Reports* (WDRs). No wonder many policy-makers in developing economies, particularly those who borrowed from the IMF and the World Bank, looked with awe and admiration at the WDRs hoping to derive some policy guidelines and the World Bank perhaps honestly believed that the WDR could provide some policy inputs. A critical look at these reports which began to be published since 1978 has been taken by Shahid Yusuf, on the eve of 30th Anniversary of WDRs, in 2009 (World Bank, 2009). This assessment finds that WDRs were mainly a summaries of inside and outside academic research, and they offered no meaningful development policy guidance.

Dr Khatkhate concludes his brilliant review of Shahid Yusuf's monograph on WDRs in the following words:

> ...It is now clear after reading this essay that the WDR far from illuminating development issues and contributing to the science of policy making is more like, to use a resonating phrase of Nandan Nilekani, a Niagara Falls of well-worn ideas and Sahara of new exciting ones.

Is this another episode of the emperor's clothes parable? One wonders.

Mahatma Gandhi Phase: 2004-2011: Rediscovering the Mahatma

The year 2005 may be said to mark a dramatic departure from the market-centred development policy or what I have broadly categorised as the Milton Friedman phase. This is when Indian policy-makers began to rediscover, as it were, Mahatma Gandhi, escaping from the trap of market fundamentalism embodied in neoliberalism. Maintaining a sustainable growth of 8 per cent for five years was, in itself, a significant achievement. But this was not enough. Inclusive growth has to be sought. It is here that India's growth story ceases to be a mere growth story: it transfigurates itself into a development drama, with community-centred development as its central theme. This takes us well beyond growth models—a failed God—to the realm of philosophy of development: it urges us to grow up from the conventional growth economics trapped in market theology to resonate to the larger concerns of holistic development including promoting of broad- based, decentralised growth which alone could facilitate access by the poor to employment, food, nutrition and health, and quality education and putting in place appropriate safety nets to reduce the vulnerability of the poor, and above all to build a value-based compassionate society. Do we need to rewrite the script of development economies?

The ambitious Bharat Nirman programme launched in 2005 with a massive investment of ₹ 1.74 lakh crore involved a time-bound programme of rural infrastructure development focussing on six subjects: roads, drinking water, irrigation, housing, electricity and telephones. In a way, this symbolises the beginning of the rediscovery of Mahatma's philosophy of rural development. This was subsequently supplemented by other flagship schemes for education and health, Sarva Shiksha Abhiyan (SSA) for education, mid-day meal scheme providing cooked meals to school children and Integrated Child Development Services (ICDS) to promote nutritional supplement to children upto the age of six years. The mid-day meal programme covers some 15 crore children.

The Mahatma Gandhi National Rural Employment Guarantee Act (NREGA), 2005, is the best thing that could have happened to the rural poor. This guarantees 100 days of employment in a year to every rural household. Today, about five crore rural households benefit from this programme. The Budget speech for 2009 summed up the new approach to development "...The UPA Government has gone for a paradigm shift for making the development process more inclusive. It involves creating entitlement barced by legal guarantee to provide basic amenities and opportunities for livelihood to vulnerable sections. Aam Admi is now the focus of all our programmes and schemes." Are we recapturing the rhythm of our old growth song with which we launched our development in 1951?

The process of discovery of the Mahatma did not stop here. The pendulum seems to have swung to the other extreme. We have become ambitious to 'feed' the bulk of the population at subsidised prices. Contrast this with the Milton Friedman phase when our policy-makers keen on abolishing food subsidy exported 'surplus' food grains. Secondly, the 'commitment deficit' which hampers our development endeavours warrants that we go beyond the textbook development economics to development philosophy designed to build a value-based society. Let us discuss these two aspects.

A Sort of Food Utopia

The culmination of these efforts is the proposed National Food Security Bill. At present, a sense of supreme complacency and total disregard for ground realities seem to characterise the approach of the authors of the National Food Security Bill (see the Document of February 21, 2011) and Food Minister K.V. Thomas. Between themselves they seem to have created a sort of 'food utopia.' The basic approach of home delivery, as it were, of a specified quantum of subsidised food grains—doorstep delivery of PDS grains is the wording in the draft Bill—is flawed. We know that many poor households do not use the PDS even when they have the necessary entitlement. Even subsidised food grains is far more important than mere legal entitlement. We therefore have to adopt a holistic approach to ensure food security.

Basically, the National Advisory Council (NAC) recommends a much higher coverage of the population to subsidised food.

Individual food entitlements proposed by NAC are: priority category 7 kg food grains per month and general category 5 kg food grains per month. It recommends a larger coverage of 72 per cent of the total population in the first phase and 78 per cent in the final phase. In the first phase, NAC estimates a total PDS requirement of 49.4 million tonnes. If we add non-PDS food grains requirements for schemes like the mid-day meals and ICDS, total requirement works out to some 58 million tonnes. The NAC feels that procurement of some 60-65 million tonnes of food grains annually 'should not be difficult.' In 2009-10 for instance, procurement of rice and wheat was around 54 million tonnes. The subsidy implication of NAC proposals is that the total subsidy would jump from the present level of ₹ 56,700 crore to ₹ 71,837 crore.

Apart from financial implications, such larger procurement and distribution of rice and wheat poses problems of logistic disaster. As it is, PDS is in a tottering condition. How does one go about increasing production and strengthening PDS? Here NAC's Explanatory Note merely lists a bunch of good intentions. There is no agenda for action. For instance, "there is a large potential for higher food grain production. India has vast untapped production reservoir in most farming systems, even with the currently available technologies."

Regarding storage of food grains—in the light of the recent criticism of insensitivity of FCI to wastage of food grains through inappropriate storage—the NAC merely states: "urgent efforts are needed to expand, improve and modernise storage of food grains in the country...." NAC also advocates 'urgent reform of PDS.'

Where do these homilies lead us? Recent researchers have provided concrete evidence of corruption in the PDS. Estimates of diversion of grains from PDS include leakages due to corruption, transport losses and losses due to spoilage. Reetika Khera has shown that the situation has deteriorated between 1990-2000 and 2007-08. At the beginning of the period, 24 per cent of the grain was diverted. In 2004-05, 54 per cent of the grains was diverted. At the end of 2007-08, 44 per cent of the grain was diverted. Although there are interstate differentials, this was the picture at the all-India level. There were seven major states whose performance was excellent, in the sense of negligible diversion. We cannot therefore label the PDS as 'dysfunctional.' One thing is quite clear. Unless this deficiency is rectified, it would not be too prudent to entrust PDS with greater responsibilities.

In the face of such evidence, Food Minister is complacent about the FCI. In a recent interview to a financial paper, he said: "but the key thing is that the machinery has to be equipped. Compared to earlier periods, the recruitment to FCI has risen by 10 per cent. We have modernised FCI godowns through computerisation. Sitting in my office, I know the quantity, quality and distribution of grain from each godown. We have put CCTV cameras to watch operations" (*Economic Times*, June 1, 2011). If the picture is so rosy, one may ask: why did the Supreme Court ask the GoI to distribute the grains free of cost to the poor, instead of allowing it to rot in the open storage of FCI? It is to the credit of NDTV, that they showed a couple of godowns of FCI where the grain was allowed to rot exposed to rain, or rats were eating away grains from one such godown. The point is that much needs to be done to improve the storage of grains in the godowns of the FCI. Entrusting PDS with greater responsibilities before raising food grains production and before streamlining FCI storage system is like putting the horse before the cart. Thus, the basic approach of NAC to food security is flawed. Providing food security does not mean that Government should produce and deliver a stipulated quantity of food grains at subsidised prices to targeted households, as the NAC proposals seem to suggest. The magnitudes involved in such operations are so forbidding that it may result in logistic disaster. What is required is creating an environment which enables households to purchase food grains through employment generation, moderating open market prices of rice and wheat, and by streamlining marketing arrangements of some items like fruits and vegetables. If public sector banks can use business correspondent (BC) model, there is no reason why FCI cannot use private trade to reach targeted households. Private and public sector participation should be an essential ingredient of a well-designed food security model. Protecting the vulnerable sections of the population through say mid-day meals or child nutrition programmes would, of course, continue to be the exclusive responsibility of public sector institutions.

Building a Value-based and Compassionate Society

This brief critical review of India's development drama over the last two decades brings us back to the larger concerns of society. Basically, we have seen that building development models or conducting econometric exercises is not the best way to generate practical policy prescriptions. Country-specific issues need to be addressed. The key to success of development in a particular country lies in the answer to the question: What ails development? In India, we have seen that 'commitment deficit' haunts many of our development endeavours. It is here that development economics spreads its arms into the broader area of development philosophy. As Ricupero Rubans puts it: "we should never forget the economy is not something that is beyond our control. The market has to be our servant, not our master. The economy is not like the planetary system or the genetic code; something that is given once and for all and which one cannot alter; it is a product of culture, it is a product of human choices; of choice of values. That is why we have to choose the right values and put competition exactly in the balance with other values and decide what are the higher values for us. We have to particularly provide people with tangible reasons to hope for the future" (Reddy, 2010). This takes back to the Mahatma.

Mahatma Gandhi had distilled the core of Indian philosophy from our ancient scriptures and evolved his own philosophy. In addition to basic needs of the common man being the first charge on the society's resources, he had another important ingredient: the concept of trusteeship. We should hold our wealth as trustees and not as exclusive owners, so that this wealth is available for sharing by others who need it most. Dr Swaminathan would like to add intellectual property rights as well to the concept of wealth.

From times immemorial, Indian philosophy has maintained that the all-round development of a society is best achieved through betterment of individuals which no doubt includes economic well-being but extends well beyond it. Social conscience must be inculcated among individuals through education at all stages and also professional training. All individuals must be sensitised, at their young age itself, to abject poverty, the squalor, disease, ignorance and illiteracy that surround us. They must begin to think in terms of what is our *dharma* or duty towards alleviating some of the infirmities that affect our less fortunate fellow human beings. Some Asian countries, recently, have introduced in school textbooks lessons on corruption. But that is a narrow and negative concept. More positively, we must aim at building a holistic concept of the right conduct.

One of the ancient scriptures of India the *Brihadaranyaka Upanishad* enjoins us that our life must be guided by the following three Das—*Damya*, that is control yourself, *Datta*, that is give to others, and *Dayadhwam*, that is be compassionate. Thus, we must practice self-control, charity and compassion. Collectively, these three characteristics constitute 'development conscience' (Mujumdar, 2007). Building up such conscience among all sections of the population would go a long way towards evolving a compassionate society—an ideal which the Mahatma sought to achieve. We must add this ingredient to our development approaches.

References

Dixit, Avinash (2006). "Evaluating Recipes for Development Success", *World Bank Policy Research Paper* 3859, The World Bank, Washington, D.C., U.S.A., March.

Khan, H.R. (2010). "Issues and Challenges in Indian Agriculture Bankers Perspectives", *RBI Bulletin*, October.

Khatkhate, Deena (2009). "Reprise of the Canons of Development Economics", *Economic and Political Weekly* 44(46): 31. November 11.

Mujumdar, N.A. (2005). *Risk Philosophy: An Enquiry into Risk and Uncertainties in Agriculture and the Role of Credit*. Monograph prepared for NABARD.

———. (2007). "The Development Conscience Factor", included in the book *Inclusive Growth*.

———. (2011). "Macro Economic Policy Mix and Micro Finance Institutions", in N.A. Mujumdar and M.G. Shirahatti (eds.), *Rethinking on Micro Finance*. Mumbai: Himalaya Publishing House.

Mujumdar, N.A. and Uma Kapila (2007). *Indian Agriculture in the New Millennium*. New Delhi: Academic Foundation.

Reddy, Y.V. (2010). *Life after Global Financial Crisis*, (Occasional Publication 14, NW). New Delhi: India International Centre.

Reserve Bank of India (2007). *Report on Currency and Finance, 2005-06*. Mumbai: RBI. p.159.

Sharma, Anand (2007). *Gandhian Way: Peace, Non-violence, and Empowerment*. New Delhi: Academic Foundation.

Shylendra, H.Y. (2010). "The New Methods of Poverty Assessment and Reduction: The Muddle and the Trap of Neoliberalism", *Working Paper*, Institute of Rural Management, Anand, December.

World Bank (2008). *The Growth Report: Strategies for Sustained Growth and Inclousive Development*. Washington D.C.: Commission on Growth and Development.

Yusuf, Shahid, Angus Deaton, Kemal Dervis, William Easterley, Takatoshi Ito and Joseph E. Stiglitz (2009). *Development Economics through the Decades. A Critical Look at 30 Years of the World Development*. Washington, D.C.: World Bank.

Presidential Address at the 71st Annual Conference of the Indian Society of Agricultural Economics organised by the University of Agricultural Sciences, Dharwad, Karnataka, November 3, 2011.

2

Kalam's Development Pilgrimage

IN this book written jointly with Srijan Pal Singh, former President A.P.J. Abdul Kalam seeks to evolve a sustainable development system of PURA-Provision of Urban Amenities in Rural Areas—by harnessing the potential energies of the rural masses (target 3 bn). PURA is an amalgam of technologies, and people—their traditional skills, and entrepreneurial spirit aimed at achieving sustainable development which is financially viable, and socially equitable and eco-friendly.

This is not a learned discourse on development models or theory. In a way, Kalam takes us on a conducted pilgrimage of development across concretely demonstrating how development is triggered in a myriad of ways. It may be the development of irrigation in a desert or improving crop yields in a backward state or promoting dairying-centred rural development.

Kalam gives us insights into how these success stories were triggered: the leadership at the grass roots may have come from a religious institution or an NRI-donor. But the result is rural resurgence. In fact the state and central governments, and the Planning Commission must study these success stories of micro enterprises so that they can replicate such enterprises in similarly situated circumstances: Rural resurgence does not mean merely establishment of a spectacularly big projects. It means facilitating blooming of millions of flowers with the help of leadership at the ground level. These micro enterprises may not accelerate farm growth in the immediate run: but they promote broad-based decentralised growth which can effectively tackle hunger and poverty.

Let us begin with irrigation in a desert Pokhran. After conducting the nuclear test, Kalam was returning and on the way stopped at Bhadariya, a small place in the middle of the desert. Here the *ashram* of Baba Sri Bhadariya Maharaja has done wonders for the community. There was a plethora of problems of poverty, hunger, health care and malnutrition. Water was very scarce. With the cooperation of villagers, the *ashram* executed a mission of greening the area and planted lakhs of trees. Tube wells were dug up and agriculture was initiated, with special steps taken to conserve water.

The villagers started providing fodder to the *ashram's* 1,000 discarded cows. The *ashram* has developed a special method of treating such stray cows and they have become productive. The *ashram* offers free milk and butter to the needy. It provides knowledge on naturopathy and herbal medicines to the rural folk and for treatment of cattle. Thus, Bhadariya and its 70 villages have become resurgent. Literally a desert has been transformed into a land flowing with milk. Visitors like Kalam are served a large glass of milk. A small dedicated band of workers have promoted, using local and traditional knowledge, water management, cattle rearing, fodder management, and so on.

Take the case of Bihar. An experiment carried out by the Technology Information, Forecasting and Assessment Council (TIFAC) showed that the paddy yield could be increased from two tonnes per hectare to 5.8 tonnes and that of wheat from 0.9 tonnes to 2.6 tonnes.

Addressing the Bihar Assembly in March 2006, Kalam urged them to adopt this system-oriented approach in 38 Bihar districts so the state could triple its paddy and wheat crops.

Dr M.R. Raju, a well-known nuclear scientist working in America, has set up a Mahatma Gandhi Memorial Medical Trust in his native village Pada Amiram in Andhra Pradesh. Within a decade this has brought about a great change among the people who focused on uplifting the children in the 3-5 age group, and brought down the dropout rate of school going children from 70 per cent to less than 30 per cent.

In the dairying sector, we know about the success story of Anand. Here we have an account of Warana in Kolhapur. The Warana Milk Cooperative has about 20,000 producers. The cooperative has brought about all-round development of the area. Kalam's total dedication to rural development has been demonstrated in another case—while he was President, he invited 6,000 farmers to Rashtrapati Bhavan on March 23, 2007.

The farmers were shown herbal garden which includes *Jatropha*, the diesel producing plant, the spiritual garden and the nutrition garden. The farmers were shown organic farming and biodiversity park and the commercial aspects of various plants and herbs were spelt out to them by experts. This is perhaps a rare case of the President playing the role of an extension agency.

As it is, innovative and progressive farming practices have been adopted by farmers. The National Innovation Foundation (NIF) has compiled data and information on these practices. Areas where the rainfall is poor or where the land remains flooded for long, mountain regions and forest areas are the most suitable for organic food farming. The NIF has reported over 240 combinations of herbal pesticides being used in different parts of the country. There are many cost-effective solutions found by farmers. For instance, planting lady's fingers (*bhindi*) as a border crop prevents cotton crops being attacked by pests, which are, instead, attracted to the flowers of the lady's fingers and the cotton crop grows well.

"This is an important zero-cost solution since 40 per cent of the pesticides in use in this country are for protecting cotton crops," says Kalam. I have come across the successful production of organic paddy in many parts. In one of the districts, 2,400 farmers joined together to cultivate organic paddy in 2,500 acres of wet land and they realised a productivity of 6.25 tonnes per hectare, which is on par with international standards.

The impression one gets from the media is the rural sector is a somnolent, sleepy area where nothing much happens: they hear the news of farmers' suicides. This book provides an ample evidence to show rural community is vibrant and there is resurgence triggered by several factors. Our policy-makers should identify these innovations and try to harness the energies of the masses for the mainstream development.

Finally, the book also makes a subtle point about the end objectives of development. In Delhi, Kalam was told that the tsunamis had engulfed many parents and rendered children orphans.

He asked the Nicobar tribal leaders "When I visited Andaman I saw three orphanages, built after the tsunami. What about Nicobar?" Kalam was told that there were no orphans here.

"The children who have been left without surviving parents, after the tsunami, are indeed children of every home. We do not need orphanages. Our own homes are taking care of these children. After all, we are one big family on this island."

Not long ago Gandhiji exhorted us to evolve a value-based compassionate society. Nicobar leaders should be congratulated for having achieved this goal. There are no orphans in a compassionate society.

3

Economic Growth

The God that Failed

THE Elusive Quest for Growth was the title of a book written in 2002 by William Easterly, a former World Bank economist. The same title perhaps remains appropriate for *The Growth Report: Strategies for Sustained Growth and Inclusive Development*, published by the World Bank (WB) in 2008.

The *Theory of Economic Growth* by Arther Lewis in 1957 became a classic in what later emerged as the discipline of development economics. This pioneering work is regarded as belonging to the same genre as Adam Smith's *Wealth of Nations* (1776). In the subsequent 55 years, we have built up a mountain of literature on growth and development contributed by academicians and the World Bank (WB) and United Nations Conference on Trade and Development (UNCTAD). Are we any wiser today in terms of providing a workable blueprint for growth and development to a developing country?

This exercise of preparing growth models and deriving policy inputs from such models was exciting and raised great hopes for redeeming poor countries from the state of underdevelopment. In the final analysis, poverty and hunger are an affront to a civilised society. In retrospect, it is legitimate to ask: How does one explain the alarming increase in the dimensions of hunger world-wide? According to Food and Agriculture Organization (FAO) estimates, the number of undernourished at 923 mn in 2007 was higher by 80 mn then the figure in 1990-1992, the base period for the World Food Summit (WFS) hunger reduction target. Is developing economics a failed God?

The disillusionment with development economics is not only with theoretical constructs but also with development policy. The Nobel Laureate Robert Solow made the famous observation that often all the discussions on the sources of growth and development end in a blaze of sociology. The 'technological change residual' so-called because it is part of the growth that cannot be explained by identifiable factors like capital and labour remained large. We have today moved well beyond Solow.

The WB-sponsored Commission on Growth and Development which submitted its report in June 2008 clearly demonstrates that our basic approach to development was perhaps flawed. The commission's main recommendations stem from an investigation into the empirical experience of 13 countries which recorded an average annual gross domestic product (GDP) growth of 7 per cent for 25 years or longer since 1950. These countries were Bostwana, Brazil, China, Hong Kong, Indonesia, Japan, the Republic of Korea, Malaysia, Malta, Oman, Singapore, Taiwan and Thailand. The commission also adds that India and Vietnam were on their way to joining this group. Distilling the empirical experience of these 13 countries, the commission comes up with five essential ingredients for faster and sustained growth: (i) these countries fully exploited the world economy; (ii) they maintained macro economic stability; (iii) they mustered high rates of saving and investment; (iv) they let markets allocate resources; and (v) they had committed, credible and capable governments.

So far so good. Can these ingredients help us to draw up blueprints for growth and development of other poor countries? The report reveals: "But it is hard to know how to replicate these characteristics." This is the tragedy of development economics. The commission admits that there is no generic formula for growth. In retrospect, it is thus clear that attempts by economists like Solow to capture the essentials of growth in a mathematical or econometric formula were misdirected. At the policy level, we may turn to the WB. When Robert McNamara launched a crusade for poverty eradication as the main goal of the WB, the WB began to articulate its development vision through its *World Development Reports* (WDRs). No wonder many policy-makers in developing countries looked with awe and admiration at WDRs hoping to derive some policy guidelines and the WB honestly believed the WDR could provide some policy inputs: A critical look at these WDRs which began to be published since 1978 has been taken by Shahid Yusuf in 2009, on the eve of 30th anniversary of WDRs. This assessment finds that WDRs were mainly summaries of inside and outside academic research and that they offered no meaningful development policy guidelines.

It is thus clear that building development models or conducting econometric exercises is not the best way to generate practical policy prescriptions. In fact larger concerns of society have now been brought into sharp focus. The global financial and economic crisis of 2008 was ferocious and it has dramatically changed the institutional and policy-making landscape. We have arrived at a moment in world economic history, when the disillusionment with centrally planned economies is matched by the loss of faith in the capitalist system, led by unbridled market forces. Do we now need to rewrite the script of development economics? This takes us well beyond the mechanistic growth models to the realm of philosophy of economic development.

These larger concerns of society are articulated by Ricupero Rubans as follows: "We should never forget the economy is not something that is beyond our control. The market has to be our servant, not our master. The economy is not like the planetary system or the genetic code; something that is given once and for all and which one cannot alter; it is a product of culture, it is a product of human choices; of choice of values. The is why we have to choose the right values and put competition exactly in balance with other values and decide what are the higher values for us. We have particularly provide people with tangible reasons to hope for the future."

This takes us back to Mahatma Gandhi. Gandhi had distilled the core of Indian philosophy from our ancient scriptures and evolved his own philosophy. Basic human needs should have the first claim on society's resources and the society has an obligation to arrange its economic affairs in a manner that the needs of all its members are met. Secondly we should hold our wealth as trustees and not as exclusive owners, so that this wealth is available for sharing by others who need it most.

4

Reinventing Development Economics

I had an occasion to write in a paper that development economics is a failed God. This is true both in terms of theoretical constructs and policy inputs. Attempts by economists like Robert Solow to capture the essential of growth in a mathematical or econometric formula were misdirected. Today the World Bank (WB)-sponsored Commission on Growth and Development asserts that there is no generic formula for growth. Secondly, a recent critical appraisal of the much-touted WB's *World Development Reports* (WDRs) has revealed that these were empty vessels offering little meaningful development policy guidelines (November 28, 2011).

It is gratifying to note that ground experience has humbled at least some of the self-appointed dispensers of development wisdom and led to some soul-searching. In a seminal paper "Shifting Patterns of Economic Growth and Rethinking Development", the WB has frankly confessed the infirmities of development economics as it has evolved so far and has come up with some suggestions for reinventing development economics and also making the WB a more relevant institution to help developing countries. "Unfortunately, development economics has not always provided useful policy guidance in the past and it may be unable to do so in the future as well."[1] Indian policy makers would greatly benefit from reading this paper, because at least some of them seem continue to be haunted by the ghosts of the conventional market theology of IMF (International Monetary Fund)/ WB.

1. Lin, Justin Yifu and David Rosenblaft (2012). "Shifting Patterns of Economic Growth and Rethinking Development", *Policy Research Working Paper* 6040. World Bank. April.

The basic flaw in our approach to development was that broad prescriptions were formulated to solve the problems of developing countries as a group and these prescriptions used the developed countries as a reference point. Waves of economic thought focused on blindly initiating and opening these economies to the developed world. No wonder these one-size-fits all policy prescriptions proved to be unsuccessful. The so-called Washington Consensus was a glaring example of such flaws. The focus was on liberalising markets and balancing budgets. The Washington Consensus advised the developing countries to adopt 'the idealised advanced countries institutions, namely free markets' without paying attention to individual country's specifics. Appropriate institutions may differ depending on the level of development of a particular country. These implied establishing a strong system of property rights, opening the economy to trade, privatising state-owned enterprises and establishing broadly free markets through deregulation. The outcome was disastrous. As John Williamson puts it, the Washington Consensus came to be perceived as "a set of neoliberal policies that have been imposed on hapless countries by the Washington-based international financial institutions and have led them to crisis and misery."

The countries that successfully accelerated their growth did not follow this approach. China is a prime example. Instead of wholesale privatisation of state-owned enterprises, the government continued its ownership and gave them preferential access to subsidised credit. The government also allowed some private enterprises to enter into competition. Market theologists predicted China would collapse but instead, China has been the most dynamic economy over the past three decades.

The WB deserves to be commended for its candid confessions of how flawed policy prescriptions, based on flawed development economics theory, were dished out to developing countries. One important outcome of these discussions is that development economics has to be reinvented, if it is to remain policy relevant. The paper advances one more important reason why such reinvention is warranted.

Multipolar Growth of the Global Economy

There are two dimensions of this phenomenon. First, the G7 dominance on the global economy declined sharply during the first decade of the 21st century. This is due to the fast growth of large dynamic emerging economies—the 'BRICs' countries (Brazil, Russia, India and China). The G7 share of global GDP declined rapidly from 45 per cent to 37 per cent from 2000 to 2009. This has caused a dramatic shift in the balance of economic power. Second, economic interactions between emerging markets have increased at an even faster pace than they have between high-income countries and developing countries. This is 'south-south' globalisation. As growth poles emerge in the developing countries, one way that more rapid growth could be sustained is through increased 'south-south' globalisation. The theories that originated in developed countries attempt to explain growth on the same lines: as such they are not necessarily relevant to developing countries. Most developing countries that followed the dominant development theories to design development policies failed to develop. There is ample rationale for rethinking economic development on a more democratic basis, that is to build on developing countries own ideas and experience. China is a case in point. It is argued Chinese economists had a natural comparative advantage in understanding their own unique development experience. This is equally true of other developing countries like India. Thoughts or ideas for developing countries development are likely to come increasingly from the developing countries themselves. This is captured in the phrase 'democratise development economics'. As WB President Robert Zoellick explains:

> With the end of the outdated concept of a Third World, the First World must open itself to competition in ideas and experience. The flow of knowledge is no longer North to South, West to East, rich to poor.
>
> Rising economies bring new approaches and solutions. We see as India advises Africa on dairy farming, as China learns from Africa about effective community-driven development approaches in Ghana and Nigeria, as the US learns from China about high-speed railways. This is no longer about the Washington Consensus. One cannot have a consensus about political economy from one city applying to all.

This is experience regarding what is working—in New Delhi, in Sao Paulo, in Beijing, in Cairo and Accra. Out of experience may come consensus. But only if it is firmly grounded—and broadly owned.

5

Home-Grown Green Revolution

IT has become fashionable to harp on the theme that a second green revolution can alone ensure food security. Hence, our policy-makers' high profile initiatives—the India-US collaboration on agricultural technology. The joint statement of Prime Minister Manmohan Singh and President Barack Obama, issued on 8th November, 2010, at the end of the latter's visit to India, mentions the decision "to work together to develop, test, and replicate transformative technologies to extend food security, as part of the Evergreen Revolution."

The first green revolution was achieved through a genetic breakthrough in seed technology, a technology which was accessible to all. A number of inventions of high-yielding varieties of seeds took place under the auspices of publicly-funded research institutions. But today the intellectual property rights of genetically modified (GM) seeds are held by the Monsantos, Duponts and Dows. These are purely agribusiness corporates aiming at maximising their profits.

In this article I argue that there are more mundane and less glamorous alternatives to attaining food and nutrition security. One does not have to look to the US to increase the levels of yields of our crops. Under the existing farming system, current level of farm technology and farm management practices, it is feasible to raise farm productivity levels. The gap between the yields in our agriculture research centres at the state level and at actual farm level is quite wide. For example, in the case of wheat it is 84 per cent for Madhya Pradesh; for rice, over 100 per cent for Assam, Bihar, Chhattisgarh and Uttar Pradesh; for soyabean, 185 per cent in Karnataka; and for sugarcane it is 167 per cent in Madhya Pradesh. Hence if we can bridge these yield gaps, we can increase production by 50 per cent. In other words, by appropriate policy thrusts, we can usher in a home-grown second green revolution.

At present, there is a surfeit of scholarship on agricultural development modalities at the macro level discourses. But these are not being translated into success stories at the ground level because there seems to be a disconnect between macro level discourses and their implementation at the ground level. Such disconnect is due to what one might call 'commitment deficit' on the part of both policy makers and development administration. This point can be substantiated with the most conspicuous example of watershed development.

Watershed Development

Future agricultural growth will have to be necessarily water-centric and what better alternative can there be than watershed development? I regard it as the mother of all water management modes. It should have been accorded the same priority as nuclear power. Watershed development projects, both micro and macro, hold out great promise for future agricultural growth. The potential area to be covered is huge, with about 60 per cent of the area under crops being rainfed. Capital investment is modest, the projects are labour intensive and do not require much technical know-how. By its very nature, growth under watershed development is 'inclusive'.

Yet, why despite all the sound and fury, have we not made any appreciable progress? For instance, the Macro Management of Agriculture (MMA) assistance during 2010-11 has been used to treat a mere 300,000 hectares of land under the National Water Development Project for Rainfed Areas (NWDPRA).

In fact, watershed development programmes have a fairly long history. It was in 1986 that NWDPRA was introduced in 99 districts in 16 states. What has happened in the subsequent quarter century? The Government of India issued in 2008, 'The Common Guidelines for Watershed Development Projects', the first set of guidelines that apply to watershed development projects across three ministries—Ministry of Rural Development, Ministry of Agriculture and Ministry of Environment and Forests. Trust the bureaucracy to mystify, sometimes with a little help from academicians, a perfectly simple and workable growth tool! We have had scholarly discourses on watershed development like the Parthasarathy Committee Report. But where are the results? Even in a progressive state like Maharashtra, the proportion of area covered by micro watershed development to the total eligible area is not significant.

It is necessary to demystify the whole approach to watershed development. Considering the humble animal—watershed development—the punditry and complexity of the 'guidelines' mentioned above is astounding. In contrast, look at the success stories of individual initiatives. In Maharashtra, Anna Hazare's Ralegaon Siddhi project has now become part of folklore of watershed movement. A more recent case is that of Hirwe Bazar, a drought-prone, poverty-stricken village about 100 kilometres from Pune. The efforts of one man, Popatrao Pawar, have converted this village into a model village. The International Groundwater Association has given this village the International Groundwater Management Award. Neither Hazare nor Pawar could have read and appreciated the erudition and comprehensiveness of the 'guidelines' referred to above. Yet they were able to evolve their own region- and location-specific models and emerge as the new Schumpeterian heroes of agricultural growth and rural development. There may be similar leaders in Gujarat, Rajasthan and elsewhere. It may be useful to produce the growth profiles of these successful stories so that we may be able to replicate them on a large scale.

The mid-term appraisals of plans of relevant states should have contained a separate section on the progress of watershed development projects. Alas, this is not so. All this shows 'commitment deficit' on the part of policy makers and the development administration.

President Kalam's Model

Rural development is a much wider concept than agricultural development. It involves education, health and nutrition of the rural population. It also involves development of allied activities, livestock, horticulture and so on.

In a book the former President of India A.P.J. Abdul Kalam seeks to evolve a sustainable development system of Provision of Urban Amenities in Rural Areas (PURA) by harnessing the potential energies of the rural masses. PURA is an amalgam of technologies and people—their traditional skills and entrepreneurial spirit aimed at achieving sustainable development, which is financially viable, socially equitable and eco-friendly.

This is not a learned discourse on development models or development theory. But the insights provided by the discussion in the book do enlighten us on how to facilitate blooming of thousands of flowers with the help of leadership at the ground level.

Let us begin with irrigation in the desert, Pokhran is deep in the Thar Desert in Western India. President Kalam was returning after conducting the nuclear test and on the way stopped at Bhadariya, a small village in the middle of the desert. Baba Sri Bhadariya Maharaja's *ashram* has done wonders for the community here. The villagers suffered problems of poverty, hunger, health care and malnutrition. Water was very scarce. With the cooperation and support of the villagers, the *ashram* executed a mission of greening the area and planted hundreds of thousands of trees. Tube wells were dug and agriculture was initiated, with special steps taken to conserve water. The villagers started providing fodder to the *ashram's* approximately 1,000 cows. In turn, the *ashram* offers free milk and butter to the needy. Thus, Bhadariya and some surrounding 70 villages have become resurgent.

Take the case of Bihar, a relatively backward state. An experiment carried out by the Technology Information Forecasting and Assessment Council (TIFAC) demonstrated that the yield of paddy could be increased from 2 tonnes per hectare to 5.8 tonnes and that of wheat from 0.9 tonnes per hectare to 2.6 tonnes. Addressing the Bihar Assembly in March 2006, President Kalam requested them to adopt this system-oriented approach in all the 38 districts of Bihar so that the state could triple its paddy and wheat crops.

M.R. Raju, a well-known nuclear scientist working in America, has set up the Mahatma Gandhi Memorial Medical Trust in his native village, Pada Amiram, Andhra Pradesh. Within a decade this has brought about a great change in the lives of the people. The trust focuses on the upliftment of children in the age group of 3 to 5 years. This has brought down the dropout rate of children in schools from 70 per cent to less than 30 per cent.

In the area of dairying, we generally read about the success story of Anand. There is equally the account of Warana Milk Cooperative in Kolhapur district. The cooperative has about 20,000 milk producers, and cover a sugar factory, banking and retail services. The cooperative has brought about all-round development of the area.

President Kalam's total dedication to rural development is well known. When he was President, he invited 6,000 farmers from all over the country to Rashtrapati Bhavan on March 23, 2007. The farmers were shown the herbal garden which includes Jatropha, a diesel producing plant, the spiritual garden, the nutrition garden and the biodiversity park. The farmers were shown organic farming and the commercial aspects of various plants and herbs were outlined by experts from leading agricultural universities. This is perhaps a rare case of a President playing the role of an extension agency! How we wish that other leaders—political, religious, intellectual—would show the same degree of involvement in development. That is the best method of promoting a resurgent India!

It is not as if innovative and progressive farming practices have not been adopted by farmers. The National Innovation Foundation (NIF) has compiled data and information on these practices. Areas with poor rainfall or where the land remains flooded for long periods of time, mountainous regions and forest areas are the most suitable for organic food farming. The NIF has reported over 240 combinations of herbal pesticides being used in different parts of the country. There are many cost-effective solutions found by farmers. For instance, planting lady's fingers (*bhindi*) as a border crop prevents cotton crops being attacked by pests (the pests are attracted to the flowers of the lady's fingers, leaving the cotton crop to grow well). This is an important zero-cost solution since 40 per cent of the pesticides in use in this country are for protecting cotton crops. In one district, 2,400 farmers joined together to cultivate organic paddy in 2,500 acres of wetland in their *panchayat* area and they realised a productivity of 6.25 tonnes per hectare, which is at par with international standards.

We do not look for imported farm technology. If we have not made significant progress in accelerating agricultural growth it is because our policy makers and development administration have not paid adequate attention to critical projects like watershed development, which is not a glamorous undertaking. We must begin to 'dirty' our hands with these mundane projects. The Reserve Bank of India's (RBI) *Report on Trend and Progress of Banking in India, 2010-11*, exhorts bankers to 'think global but act local'. This should be our mantra for agricultural and rural development. Secondly, rural development extends far beyond agricultural development. This is where 'let a thousands flowers bloom' approach seems to be appropriate. There are several Schumpeterian heroes who have emerged in the rural sector demonstrating what can be achieved in different fields. Effectively incorporating several innovations, including the zero-cost solutions referred to above; into the blueprint of area-specific development plans can bring about a home-grown green revolution.

6

Medium-term Prospects for Growth

THE Reserve Bank of India (RBI) has always provided an expert assessment of the growth prospects of the economy for the ensuing years. But these are essentially exercises in short-term forecasting. But what is special about the *Annual Report 2010-11* is that it has provided a brief discourse on medium-term challenges for growth of the economy. Unfortunately, the Report has not attracted adequate attention from the media. The issues raised in the discourse need to be discussed widely. But before we take up the issues, a word about the outlook for the economy for 2011-12. After the above trend, GDP growth of 8.5 per cent in 2010-11 is expected to decelerate to around 8 per cent in 2011-12. Crop prospects remain good, and growth prospects for agriculture are promising, though these rates of growth would be lower than that of last year because of high base. The outlook, for industrial sector remains rather uncertain with the downside risks outweighing the upside risks. The downside risks include failling business confidence in the face of global uncertainties, firm commodity prices amidst inflationary pressures and tightening of monetary policy. The robustness of the services sector which accounts for more than 65 per cent of GDP would continue to support the growth process. Inflation would remain high and moderate to about 7 per cent by March 2012. The global uncertainty sticks inflation, hardening interest rates, and relatively lower agricultural growth would moderate growth in 2011-12.

Among the challenges posed for medium-term growth, let us discuss the following three: agricultural growth, savings rate and infrastructure financing.

a) Agricultural Growth: Agricultural growth is central to sustaining high GDP growth. The immediate challenge is to raise agricultural growth from the present trend rate of around 3 per cent to 4 per cent.

This would require a judicious use of technology, institutional reforms including those designed to provide incentives for supply response and better input use. The Report faithfully lists all the text-bookish measures. What is amusing is that it takes a rather romanticised view of agricultural growth as is reflected in the following paragraph: "India is a knowledge economy with a strong technology base. Yet it has not fully reaped the dividends from technology. For instance, substantial productivity enhancements are possible on the farm sector through better adoption of technology aided by incentives and institutional improvement. Large scale introduction of Precision Farming Techniques involving GIS and Remote Sensing, combined with local specific fertigation practices, better cultivars and optimum water management can go a long way to improve farm productivity on a sustainable basis."

Nobody disagrees with the statement. The point is we must look at ground realities and draw up our priorities. Why have we over the years, deemphasised the role of the village level extension worker? How should we revive the institution? Watershed holds out great promise for agricultural growth. Though we initiated these programmes as long back as in 1986, why have we not made appreciable progress? Ministries, not one but three, are busy now in issuing guidelines for watershed development projects! In the past, public sector banks (PSBs) have played a proactive role in providing extension services. Can we revive this practice? One would expect that RBI as a policy making institution would provide some concrete policy inputs at the ground level. Instead, it has chosen to wax eloquent on the high-profile agricultural technology.

b) Saving Rate: The Report underlines the imperative need to raise gross domestic saving (GDS) by about 5 percentage points from the level of 33.7 per cent in 2009-10, to be able to achieve the Twelfth Five Year Plan (2012-2017) growth target of say, 9 per cent. In this context, it is important to note that household sector savings have remained stagnant as a per cent of GDP since 2000-01. One reason may be that we have promoted consumerism in the post-reform period. An equally important reason is that we have promoted gold imports. For instance, the value of gold imports soared from $14.47

billion in 2008-09 to $33.95 billion in 2010-11, more than doubled. As a per cent of GDP, gold imports have risen from 1.5 to 2 during this period. In other words, there has taken place de-financialisation of household savings. Investment in gold as a hedge against inflation may be good for individuals or households. For the system as a whole, this is regressive because resources are being diverted from productive assets to unproductive asset. Liberalisation of import of gold is welcome up to a point but we have gone to the other extreme. Today, there are more jewellery shops than grocery shops not only in metro cities but also in smaller towns. It is a blunder to promote this trend. RBI could have analysed this factor as one of causes of stagnation of household sector financial savings and suggested some policy measures to dis-incentivise large-scale gold imports. But it has not even broached this topic.

c) Financing of Infrastructure: According to Planning Commission's estimates, during the Twelfth Plan (2012-2017) investment requirement for infrastructure development is of the order of US $1 trillion. This poses a mammoth financing task. The financing issue relates not only to bridge the financial gap but also to ensure commercially viable funding. In recent years, the banking system's credit to this sector has witnessed high growth, despite the risk of asset-liability mismatch. The Report discusses various modes of financing including increasing participation of the private sector. But there are no innovative ideas to enhance fiscal revenues. Since infrastructure development is critical to promote medium-term growth of GDP, we should explore all possible avenues. One such possible source is a tax on dividends. At present dividends received by individuals are totally exempt from income tax without any limit. Thus persons receiving thousands of crores of rupees of dividend income are totally free from income tax, while those earning modest incomes from professions are taxed. It is high time that this fiscal inequality is corrected.

Thus while RBI's discourse on constraints on medium-term growth prospects is indeed welcome, what is sought to be emphasised here is that such discussion should be focused on ground realities to yield some concrete policy inputs.

7

Even a 7 per cent Growth is Commendable

THE Mid-year Economic Review presented to the parliament scaled down the GDP forecast for 2011-12 to 7.25 per cent to 7.50 per cent from the 9 per cent projected in the budget. The stock market reacted sharply with the Sensex declining by 275 points to 16,213. Is the sharp decline justified? After all against the background of the fast deteriorating global economic environment and the Eurozone crisis, even a 7 per cent growth is commendable. Here one has to look beyond GDP growth to the overall state of the economy.

The outlook for the economy is shaped by a number of factors, other than the fundamentals. First, the infirmity of policy formulation. Our policy-makers seem to be a confused lot. This is illustrated by the fact the Government had to put on hold its proposal to permit foreign direct investment (FDI) in retail. The more pertinent question is: how is it that FDI in organised retail became all of a sudden a top priority on the policy agenda? Admittedly, FDI in retail does confer some benefits to the economy. But our policy-makers began to discover new virtues in FDI in retail. The Chief Economic Adviser, Ministry of Finance, asserted that we can control inflation through FDI in retail. Since when have the standard text-books on monetary policy began to include FDI supported retail as an instrument of inflation control? One may ask. Second, there is a sizable wastage of farm produce because of lack of proper storage. Agreed, but is FDI in retail the only solution? We have been discussing this since the report of the All-India Rural Credit Survey in 1956. Why have we not been able to achieve much progress in this field? After all, there is no technology which is the exclusive preserve of the multinational corporations (MNCs) and India Inc. or even public sector undertakings (PSUs) can handle these problems effectively. Third, FDI in retail is supposed to generate a number of jobs. This is doubtful. In fact unorganised retail, by its very nature, is labour-intensive. The scope for self-employment is enormous. Ironically, the Agriculture Minister recently wrote to the Prime Minister advocating that the scale of operations under the Mahatma Gandhi National Rural Employment Guarantee Act (NREGA) should be reduced because it has resulted in the scarcity of rural labour for normal cultivation of crops. In other words, NREGA is creating labour scarcity in some areas.

In any case, experts have enough experience in forging the supply chain that links farmer-producer to the consumer. But today where are the cooperative leaders of yesteryears who built up the mighty sugar cooperatives in Maharashtra? Or Dr Kuriens who had such resounding success in the dairying industry? We have to re-discover such leaders both in the private and public sectors. The point to drive home is that if our policy-makers—irrespective of the party in power—had pursued these objectives of streamlining agricultural marketing and providing proper storing and transportation of agricultural produce, with even one-tenth of the passion with which they are now pursuing FDI supported retail, our problems would have been solved long ago. We have resources to build world-class airports but not for building storage facilities for foodgrains. It is tragic to see the foodgrains stored in the open by the FCI being eaten by rats or rotting because of rains. The other two major concerns expressed by the Mid-year Review are fiscal deterioration and slower moderation of inflation.

Though inflation is decelerating, the pace is not satisfactory. Inflation eased to 9.11 per cent in November 2011. The Government expects inflation to decline to 7 per cent by March 2011. Even this level is well above the RBI's comfort level. Without mentioning the likely outcome of fiscal deficit, the Review admits that, deficit target of 4.6 would be exceeded.

Two other developments subsequent to the release of the Review have clouded the growth outlook. First, the credibility of export data is being questioned. There has been overestimation of exports because of wrong data entry, double counting of some items of exports and malfunctioning of computer. However, what is consoling is that even after correction of these errors, export growth during April-November remains comfortable at 33 per cent. The second is rather disturbing. Data on industrial output released on December 12 showed that on a year-on-year basis, the output declined by 5 per cent. Unless this is an aberration from the trend, such sharp decline raises apprehensions regarding our ability to sustain a 7 per cent growth. As an immediate reaction the Sensex dropped by 343 points to touch 15,870. There is some tentative evidence to indicate this is an aberration. First, Manpower Groups' employment outlook survey indicates that India Inc. will continue to hire staff, although in small numbers, in the January-March 2012 quarter. Second, bank credit off-take has picked up. Outstanding loans recorded a growth, on a year-on-year basis, of nearly 18 per cent for the fortnight ended December 2, 2011. One could, therefore, hope industrial production will resume its normal growth path.

The most redeeming feature of the deceleration in inflation is that food inflation declined sharply to 4.35 per cent during the week ended December 3, 2011 from 6.6 per cent level of the previous week. Prices of vegetables, fruit and pulses softened. This should enable policy-makers to re-focus on issues relating to slowing down of growth. This change in policy stance was clearly reflected in the monetary policy of RBI Governor Dr Subbarao on December 16. Policy rates remained unchanged. Repo rate remained unchanged at 8.5 per cent after 13 successive increases. Reverse repo rate remained at 7.5 per cent. There was some anticipation that the cash reserve ratio (CRR) would be reduced: but this did not happen. However, Dr Subbarao clearly indicated: "From this point on, monetary policy actions are likely to reverse the cycle responding to the risks to growth." One would have thought that his pause in monetary tightening would give a boost to the stock market. But the Sensex declined by 345 points to 15,491. Are prophets of doom dominating the market? One should remember that stock markets are not a barometer of what transpires in the real economy.

Despite the adversarial global economic crisis, India is capable of sustaining a reasonable high growth momentum. This is because the bulk of development is financed by domestic savings. So long as India's domestic savings remain high at around 35 per cent of GDP, one need not unduly worry, about a random decline in industrial growth.

8

Gold Imports

Drag on Economy

INDIA'S recent growth story is impressive with GDP growth recording an annual average growth of 8.5 per cent during the five years 2003-2008. Even during the year 2009-10 of global meltdown, India managed to post a growth of 7.2 per cent what is the source of strength of the Indian economy? Higher rate of saving and investment. Investment as a proportion of GDP increased from 25 per cent in 2007-08 to 38 per cent in 2007-08. What is more, of this 13 percentage points increase, as much as 10 percentage points was financed domestically, through higher household, public sector and corporate savings.

Unfortunately, massive imports of gold in the more recent years seem to threaten to erode this source of strength of the economy, through their impact on household sector financial savings and on current account deficit (CAD), on balance of payments. Imports of gold and silver aggregated $50 billion in 2011-12 (April-January). This was an increase of 46 per cent over the level during the corresponding period of the previous year. These imports hovered around only $5 billion during the early 2000s. In a poor country like ours, the policy of promoting gold imports on such an alarming scale does not make any economic sense. Of course, we have promoted import of dog food from France but the amounts involved are miniscule. Our policy-makers seem at long last to have woken up to the absurdity of massive gold imports and have begun to make appropriate noises: but the voice is feeble and lacks conviction. This article seeks to show that unless gold imports are reduced drastically, these will act as a drag on the future pace of growth of the economy.

The first official admission of the dangers of import of gold on such a massive scale is reflected in the budget speech of Pranab Mukherjee on March 16, 2012. To quote the Minister: "One of the primary drivers of the current account deficit has been the growth of almost 50 per cent in imports of gold and other precious metals in the first three quarters of this year. I have been advised to strengthen steps already taken to check this trend for better results. I propose to increase basic customs duty on standard gold bars, gold coins of purity exceeding 99.5 per cent and platinum from 2 per cent to 4 per cent and on non-standard gold from 5 per cent to 10 per cent."

During the first phase of economic reforms in the 1990s, one of the most retrogressive measures introduced was liberalisation of import of gold. The annual average level of imports of gold worked out to $5 billion in the initial years. It has now risen to $50 billion—an alarming level. Import of gold is in a way a definancialisation of savings: because financial savings which could have been channeled to productive purposes would be diverted to unproductive investment in gold. Surely, the World Trade Organization (WTO) did not prescribe the liberalisation of gold imports. You can imagine what it means to fritter away $50 billion of the household sector savings in this unproductive asset.

Naturally, both savings and investment rates declined in 2010-11: savings from 33.8 per cent of GDP in 2009-10 to 32.3 per cent and investment from 36.6 per cent to 35.1 per cent. The household sector savings rate declined rather sharply from 25.4 per cent to 22.8 per cent. Within household savings, financial savings declined even more sharply: there was slower growth in bank deposits, like insurance as well as an absolute decline in investment in shares and debentures. In the Indian economy, household sector contributes the bulk of financial savings and hence such decline, if it persists, will erode the basic strength of the economy referred to at the beginning of the article.

Such massive imports of gold affected adversely the CAD on balance of payments. The CAD at 4.3 per of GDP in the third quarter of 2011-12 was significantly higher than 2.3 per cent recorded during the corresponding quarter of 2010-11. This deficit was financed by drawing down foreign exchange reserves by $4 billion in the third quarter of 2011-12.

Prudent external sector management is warranted to ensure that CAD does not widen further. In fact about 2 per cent of CAD is regarded as a safe level and anything above has to be corrected without delay. Our contemporary policy-makers should revisit the experience of the 1991 crisis when the country had foreign exchange reserves to finance only one month's imports. Already there are downside risks to India's external sector. For the first time since 2009, exports declined by 5.7 per cent in March 2012 due to poor demand from Europe. Hence the Reserve Bank of India's (RBI) document on the Indian economy recommends: "In this regard, steps need to be taken to facilitate a complete pass through of international commodity prices, especially by raising domestic prices of petroleum products, curb the demand for precious metals and accelerate reforms to attract FDI" (*Macroeconomic and Monetary Developments in 2011-12*, April 2012).

In the early phase of liberalisation, some of us had warned that such unlimited import of gold was not merely irrational but it was a blunder. At that time, imports of gold were hovering around $5 billion per annum. Of course, the warning fell on deaf ears. Today when the imports have exceeded $50 billion, the warning has proved prophetic. These imports are threatening the future course of growth itself: first, by shrinking the size of financial savings, and second by widening the CAD to unsustainable levels. One shudders to think of the 1991 crisis. Although the policy-makers—both the Ministry of Finance and RBI—seem to have recognised the problem, the measures taken are inadequate. A small rise in customs duty is unlikely to reduce gold imports. What is required is a drastic step, including a quantitative ceiling on gold imports. One hopes the authorities would not take a decade to realise the seriousness of problem and take drastic measures immediately.

9

Gold Cliff

Wisdom Dawns on RBI

THERE is a need to moderate the demand for gold imports, as ensuring external sector's stability is critical, exhorts the report, released by the Reserve Bank of India (RBI) in January 2013, of the Working Group to study the issues related to gold imports and gold loans by Non-bank Finance Companies (NBFCs). India imported a staggering quantity of 1,112 tonnes of gold at a cost of $61 billion in 2012-13. That means India now consumes about one quarter of the total global supplies of gold. This large-import bill contributes about 30 per cent of the trade deficit. The current account deficit (CAD) has deteriorated to 4.2 per cent of the gross domestic product (GDP). Normally, CAD of 2 per cent is regarded as safe and anything above this level is unsustainable. This gave the warning signal and the RBI constituted a Working Group, which submitted its report in August 2012.

In a way, the problem of gold imports assuming alarming proportions is our own creation. Prior to 1992, there was a ban on the import of gold. The Government of India started liberalising the import of gold from 1992 and permitted its import by certain nominated agencies, *viz*., Minerals and Metals Trading Corporation, Handicrafts and Handlooms Export Corporation, State Bank of India (SBI), etc. Intoxicated with the market theology of the 1990s, our policy makers have pushed India to what one might call the 'gold cliff.' The Dr Tarapore Committee on capital account convertibility also recommended in 1997 that it was essential to liberalise the import of gold. The World Trade Organization (WTO) did not ask us to liberalise the import of gold. Even the International Monetary Fund (IMF), which was a strong advocate of full convertibility, chastened by empirical experience, started to soft-pedal the issue. But those were the heady days of market theology in India. Even when gold imports were modest, at about $5 billion, I had warned that liberalising gold imports was blunder and also, the warning has proved to be prophetic. A poor country which continues to be the abode of the largest number of underfed and undernourished persons in the world, cannot afford to definancialise and invest enormous amounts of $60 to $70 billion in an unproductive asset like gold. At long last, wisdom has dawned on the RBI. If left unchecked, gold imports would play havoc with the economy, disrupting growth.

Dr K.U.B. Rao, chairman of the RBI Working Group, should be congratulated on assembling a mass of data on related issues and providing an excellent analysis of the issues involved. I am sure the report will remain as the standard reference work on gold for years to come.

What are the factors underlying the spurt in demand for gold? The price of gold, rural income distribution, the quantum of black money, the rate of return on alternate financial assets and the general price level. Returns on gold investment have outperformed other comparable assets in three of the last five years.

Here one important distinction needs to be made between returns on gold to an individual investor and returns to the community as a whole. While individuals do derive benefits from investing in gold, for the community the benefits are nil because gold does not add to the stream of national income. In this sense, it is a dead investment.

How does one go about reducing the import of gold? The conventional method is to raise the import duties on gold. In fact, the Finance Minister, in a statement made on January 2, 2013, indicated his intentions to do so. The Working Group, however, is sceptical about the measure producing the desired result because gold imports in India are price inelastic as the empirical experience shows. Nonetheless, there is justification for raising the import duties both to disincentivise gold imports and also add some revenue to the exchequer.

The Working Group has shown remarkable insight into the problem when it states: “What is critical is to ensure provision of real higher returns to investors through various financial savings products. What is also relevant is the need for banks to introduce new gold-backed financial products that may reduce or postpone the demand for gold imports. The Working Group believes that providing a real rate of higher return to investors through alternative investments holds the key to reducing the excessive demand for gold. Meanwhile, "there is also a need to increase monetization of idle gold stocks in the economy for productive purposes." The Working Group has offered a number of concrete proposals towards achieving this objective. The RBI would do well to act on these proposals promptly.

Among the proposed new gold-backed financial products designed to reduce the demand for physical gold are: Modified Gold Deposit Scheme (gold taken as a deposit is recycled for meeting domestic demand and given back at the time of maturity); Gold Accumulation Plan (the product is a saving plan catered to even small buyers of gold in which the gold imports are deferred till the time of actual delivery of gold); Gold Linked Account (the entire transaction takes place outside India and the import of gold is not involved); and Gold Pension Product (the customer surrenders gold to the bank on agreement to receive streams of monthly pension till his death).

Other important proposals put forward by the working group relate to recycling of domestic gold and monetisation of gold. Temples in India hold large quantities of gold in the form of jewellery. If the recent discovery of gold treasury of the Padmanabha temple in Thiruvananthapuram is any guide, private holdings of gold add to astronomical figures. Perhaps the heap of gold pooled from all temples may be larger than the pooled gold reserves of Central Banks of major countries in the world. It is in this sense that India is said to be a rich country inhabited by poor people. Similarly, scrap gold of some 300 tonnes is generated every year. It would be good to devise a *modus operandi* to channel at least a part of this gold into the formal financial system.

Perhaps the most important proposal in this context is the setting up of a bullion corporation or Gold Bank. The purpose of the Gold Bank is to offer a 'backstop facility' to provide refinance to institutions lending against the collateral of gold. It can also undertake retailing functions in gold, including pooling of idle gold. The Gold Bank can make purchases and sales of gold: it can issue gold bonds and collect gold stocks. It can mobilise domestic private gold holdings and deploy them for productive uses. In fact, one could think in terms of the Gold Bank employing agents—on the lines of banking correspondents—to reach potential customers in not only urban, but rural areas also. Such operations on a countrywide scale hold out great potential for mobilising domestic private gold.

Instead of the usual stock answer to ban gold imports, the Working Group has provided various alternatives to achieve the objective. Because a ban may drive gold imports to unofficial channels. In this sense, the alternatives recommended by the Working Group offer a lasting and more productive solution to tackle the problem of alarming levels of gold imports. The ball is in the RBI court now and one hopes it will respond promptly.

10

India's Growth

Inflation Dynamics

GOVERNOR, Reserve Bank of India (RBI), Dr Subbarao took another baby step and raised on June 16, 2011, the repo rate from 7.25 per cent to 7.5 per cent; and the reverse repo rate from 6.25 per cent to 6.5 per cent. Consequently, there will be an upward adjustment in the interest rate structure and commercial banks would raise their lending rates. The domestic inflation remains high at above 9 per cent in May 2011—much above the comfort zone of RBI. The upward revision of the policy rates is expected to contain inflation and anchor inflationary expectations by reining in demand side pressures.

This is the tenth time in the last 15 months that policy rates have been raised. In response, commercial banks have raised their base rates by 1.5 to 3 per cent during July 2010 and May 2011. Does such anti-inflationary policy of raising lending rates necessarily hurt growth? Governor Subbarao in his May 2011 statement, which we will discuss presently, has stated that there is such trade-off between inflation and growth. One wonders whether we are being text-bookish in assuming such trade-off. We need to analyse this growth-inflation dynamics in the India-specific context.

Let us take two examples. Foodgrains production in 2010-11 at 236 million tonnes is estimated to be the highest ever surpassing the previous peaks achieved in 2008-09. Significant increases in output of key agricultural products would help in reducing the pressure on food prices. Thus food inflation is likely to be contained. And this phenomenon is unrelated interest rates.

Second, the recent robust growth in exports, which we will discuss shortly. Export growth in recent months has been phenomenal. That is, the recent increase in lending rates, brought about by tight monetary policy, has not eroded India's international competitiveness.

Private corporate sector in India is very vocal in resisting any increase in lending rates and our policy-makers are very sensitive to corporate sector sentiments. The so-called growth-inflation dynamics is a reflection of our policy maker's sensitiveness to corporate sector concerns. The same RBI had no qualms about endorsing an interest rate of 26 per cent for micro finance institutions (MFIs).

The genesis of this growth-inflation dilemma may be traced to the accommodative monetary policy pursued by the RBI beginning September 2008. This policy, as the RBI puts it: "instilled confidence in the market participants, mitigated the adverse impact of global financial crisis on the economy and ensured that the economy started recovering ahead of most other economies" (statement of Governor Dr D. Subbarao, April 20, 2010). There was run-away expansion of non-food credit, as reflected in the incremental credit-deposit ratio sometimes exceeding 100 per cent. There was sharp recovery of growth during 2009-10, despite the worst south-west monsoon since 1972: gross domestic product (GDP) growth reverted to near trend growth of 8 per cent.

However, while the economy recovered rapidly from the growth slowdown, inflationary forces which were triggered by the supply side factors developed into wider inflationary pressures. The headline inflation, as measured by year-on-year variation in Wholesale Price Index (WPI) rose to 9.9 per cent in March 2010 exceeding RBI's baseline projection of 8.5 per cent in March 2010. Hence there was need to bring back into focus the challenge of control of inflation to ensure macroeconomic stability. The current measures of monetary tightening have to be viewed against this broader background.

High inflation rates persisted despite monetary tightening, the rate rising to higher than 9 per cent in May 2011. Thus the Annual Policy Statement of Governor Dr Subbarao, announced on May 3, 2011, underlined this important point: "The monetary policy trajectory that is being initiated in this Annual Statement is based on the following premise. Over the long run, high inflation is inimical to sustained growth as it harms investments by creating uncertainty. Current elevated rates of inflation pose significant risks to future growth. Bringing them down therefore, even at the cost of some growth in the short-run, should take precedence."

Inflation control necessarily involves raising of interest rates and high lending rates affect corporate sector growth adversely through eroding corporate sector earnings. Interestingly, exports have been growing since October 2009, and despite monetary tightening, this growth is continuing to be robust. The growth rates are astounding: 20 per cent or 40 per cent or even 100 per cent! Even making allowance for last year's low base, the growth figures are impressive. RBI experts offer the following explanations: "The robust export growth in India's exports reflects diversification of products from labour intensive manufactures to higher value-added products in engineering and petroleum sectors and to destinations across emerging markets and developing economies..." The point is higher interest costs have not eroded India's international competitiveness.

From the medium-terms perspective, control of inflation is imperative and let us not hesitate to raise interest rates, to the extent necessary. Let us not be swayed away by the corporate sector lobby of growth-inflation trade-off. Growth of the Indian economy as well as control of inflation in India are determined by a number of factors other than lending rates.

11

RBI's Prescription for Ailing Economy

THE performance of the Indian economy in 2011-12 was so disappointing that it makes us wonder whether India's growth story has come to an inglorious end. After two successive years of robust growth of 8.4 per cent, GDP decelerated sharply to 6.5 per cent—the slowest pace in nine years. Then there are twin deficits, fiscal deficit and the current account deficit (CAD). After an impressive period of fiscal consolidation during 2002-03 to 2007-08, there has been a marked deterioration in the fiscal position. The gross fiscal deficit (GFD)/GDP ratio that had declined from 5.9 per cent in 2002-03 to 2.5 per cent in 2007-08 is back at the same level. On the external front, the CAD on the balance of payments side has deteriorated. CAD has widened to unsustainable levels in 2011-12 reaching a historical high of 4.2 per cent of GDP. This is in contrast to a level of 3 per cent, on an average, during 2002-03 to 2007-08. This deterioration partly reflects the impact of higher fiscal deficits. In fact CAD of around 2 per cent is regarded as safe. Inflation remained elevated at over 9 per cent in the first eight months of 2011-12 before softening moderately in December. It has remained sticky in the range of 7 to 7.7 per cent in the subsequent period. This is despite the fact that RBI persisted with monetary tightening till October 2011.

A more disturbing trend from the medium term point of view is the decline in the average saving rate since 2008-09. The rate of savings declined from 35 per cent in 2005-06 to 2007-08 to 32.7 per cent in 2008-09 to 2010-11. Household sectors savings declined by 1 per cent during this period. In a highly analytical discourse on the economy, the *RBI Annual Report* for 2011-12, released in August, provides fresh insights into what has gone wrong and also offers some prescriptions for policy correctives.

Let us focus on the following three specific issues: role of monetary policy, widening CAD and financial inclusion.

Role of Monetary Policy

There is a general impression, created by the corporate sector particularly that RBI's monetary tightening has been a predominant factor for the slowdown in GDP growth. The corporate sector seems to believe that higher interest rates—lending rates by banks—have led to slow growth. In fact some mandarins of the Finance Ministry join the chorus of the corporate. The RBI's *Annual Report* has successfully demonstrated that this is not so. Even at the current levels of the policy rate, RBI emphasises, the real effective lending rates of banks are relatively lower in comparison with their pre-crisis levels. This shows interest rates alone cannot explain the slowdown in growth. The corporate sector is barking at the wrong tree when clamouring for lowering lending rates. It is important to appreciate what monetary policy can or cannot do. First, monetary policy can have a strong long-run impact on inflation but it can influence output in a limited way by nudging growth towards the potential. But monetary policy cannot bring about permanent or long-run changes in the levels of output, which are mainly driven by technology, productivity changes and fiscal policy through its impact on thrift and investment behaviour. Second, the adverse welfare consequences of high inflation are large. Inflation acts like a regressive tax and hurts the poor most. Consequently monetary policy will need to be carefully calibrated to the evolving growth-inflation dynamics.

In other words, fiscal policy must take on its legitimate share of responsibility both in terms of controlling inflation and stimulating growth.

Widening Current Account Deficit

The most important point that the report makes is: "For minimizing the possibility of external shocks further disrupting India's growth sustainability over the next few years it is important not only to focus on financing of CAD, but also on compressing CAD to lower manageable levels." The widening of CAD in 2011-12 was mainly due to high imports of oil and gold. In fact gold imports reached a peak of 1,000 tonnes this year. The value of gold imports constitutes about 10 per cent of total imports. When in the 1990s unbridled gold imports had been facilitated, I had argued that this is a policy blunder. The recent developments have vindicated the argument. A country which continues to be the abode of the largest number of underfed and undernourished people in the world, cannot afford to invest in an unproductive asset like gold. At long last, RBI has conceded the point. Now both Government and RBI must take immediate measures to curb the imports of gold. In a way the CAD problem seems to be a problem of our own making, as we will see.

In a different context, the case of coal is also relevant here. It is an anomaly that India with proven coal reserves of 114 billion tonnes has to import about 70 million tonnes of coal a year. A major investment initiative in India's mining sector could have changed the outlook for energy sector. The Planning Commission does not cover itself in glory by not enabling say Coal India to exploit and utilise coal reserves. The critical nature of the energy sector has not been appreciated adequately. It is an irony of economic history that our policy-makers who should have long back addressed this task head-on are busy in 2012 sorting out the 'Coalgate mess'.

Financial Inclusion

RBI has taken several measures to accelerate the process of financial inclusion: banks were required to provide 'no-frills' accounts, were asked to improve their outreach through business facilitator and business correspondent (BC) models and were given a target of reaching all the 74,414 villages with a population of over 2,000. Despite all these efforts the report proclaims: "Yet, the RBI's assessment is that the financial inclusion remains a substantially unfinished agenda", first, over 110,000 BCs are now employed but this is not a large number in the context the under-banked villages that exist. Second, the number of no-frills accounts opened by banks rose to 103 million by March 2012. But over three-fourths of these accounts are dormant.

The most disturbing feature of the whole exercise is the bankers' attitude to these accounts. Governor Subbarao is more blunt when he says: "The general impression I got is that frontline, managers treat no-frills accounts as a nuisance and low income households as an intrusion into their time and business. This is disappointing to say the least. Actually, financial inclusion should be looked upon by banks as an opportunity to build "fortune at the bottom of the pyramid." Outsourcing financial inclusion to other layers may be useful upto a point. Ultimately, these layers have to be integrated with the mainstream banking.

12

Reforms Euphoria and Growth Prospects

ONLY recently I had the occasion to write in this column: "The performance of the Indian economy in 2011-12 was so disappointing that it makes us wonder whether India's growth story has come to an inglorious end."

But look at the current euphoria about the prospects of India's growth. There have been dramatic developments in policy making during say a week beginning September 14. First, the Government increased the price of diesel by ₹ 6.2 per litre from September 14. This measure is designed to cut down the fiscal deficit which is threatening to reach or even exceed 6 per cent of GDP. The orginal target of 5.1 per cent is simply not feasible. Second, there is the package of policy reform permitting foreign direct investment (FDI) in multi-brand retail and civil aviation. Optimists expect around $16 billion of FDI would flow into retail in the next three years. Third, although the Reserve Bank of India (RBI) did not walk the whole mile with the Government by reducing policy rates, cut the cash reserve ratio (CRR) on September 17 by 25 basis points thereby releasing ₹ 17,000 crore of liquidity into the banking system. This would perhaps enable banks to ease their lending rates. In fact the State Bank of India (SBI) took the lead in cutting its base rate by 25 basis points on September 18. Taken together these measures have created a sort of euphoria in the domestic corporate sector and among foreign banks. Bombay Stock Exchange (BSE's) Sensex jumped by 443 points on September 14 to reach 18,464. This is the highest close in the last 14 months. During these two weeks foreign institutional investors (FIIs) have poured ₹ 3,000 crore in the Indian stock markets. The euphoria does not end here. Leading foreign banks are expecting a new bull phase in the stock market. This is reflected in their raising the targets for the benchmark Sensex: Deutsche Bank's target is 20,000 by December

2012; Citibank's 19,900 by June 2013 and Morgan Stanley's 23,069 by December 2013. Although international bankers are no longer a respected tribe after the global financial crisis of 2008. Indian policy-makers may like to use these optimistic projections as indicators of the economy's growth prospects. The question is to what extent is this reforms-induced exuberance rational? Walmart may walk into India but not with a development mission. You cannot fault Walmart if it claims its pound of flesh. It is too simplistic to assume that growth will ride on the back of FDI flow in the multi-brand retail. Creating an environment for larger flow of foreign funds is important no doubt but this is only a small step. The euphoria generated by the current reforms is far from justified. There are far more critical issues for accelerating growth-issues which can be tackled domestically with little help from foreign capital and advice. Our policy-makers seem to be obsessed with foreign capital and, alas, their agenda does not have space for these less glamorous, mundane critical issues. Let us illustrate these three issues in concrete terms: strength of domestic saving and investment, definancialisation of savings, and watershed development.

If India coped with the 2008 global financial crisis reasonably well, it is because of its strength of domestic saving and investment. Investment as a proportion of GDP increased from 25 per cent in 2002-03 to 38 per cent in 2007-08. Of this 13 percentage points increase, as much as 10 percentage points was financed domestically through higher household, public sector and corporate savings. What is happening today? The most disturbing trend is the decline in the average saving rate since 2008-09. The rate of savings declined from 35 per cent in 2005-06 to 2007-08 to 32.7 per cent in 2008-09 to 2010-11. Household sector savings which are very important in the overall savings rate declined by 1 per cent during this period. Our policy-makers either in the Finance Ministry or in RBI do not seem to have given serious thought to the question of restoring the savings rate to 35 per cent. Unlike in the case of developed countries, in India, household sector contributes the bulk to overall savings. What incentives we should provide to household savers to motivate them to save more? We tried to deregulate the interest rate on savings accounts but in effect most banks continue to pay 4 per cent on savings, with only a couple of banks offering 5 or 6 per cent. We have practically ignored the small saver.

Definancialisation of savings forms a sub-theme of the above subject. In the name of liberalisation, our policy-makers permitted in the 1990s unlimited imports of gold. Today its imports have reached an alarming figure of 1,000 tonnes. Its value constitutes 10 per cent of total imports. A poor country cannot afford to invest such an enoromous amount in an unproductive asset like gold. At long last, RBI has conceded the point and has made a plea for reduction in the quantum of gold imports. This measure will not only reduce the balance of payments current account deficit (CAD) but simultaneously release large financial resources for productive investment.

The nitty-gritty of growth also involves more mundane issues like watershed development. Future agricultural growth in India will have to necessarily be water-centric. I regard watershed development as the mother of all water management modes. With about 60 per cent of the area under crops being rainfed, the potential area to be covered by watershed development projects is large. Capital investment is modest and projects are labour-intensive. By its very nature, growth under watershed development is 'inclusive'. Despite all these positive features why is it that we have not made any significant progress in this field? We initiated such programmes in 1986 and what has happened in the subsequent quarter century? The Government issued in 2008 "The Common Guidelines for Watershed Development Projects"! Of course there are success stories of individual initiatives. In Maharashtra, Anna Hazares' Ralegaon Siddhi has now become part of the folklore of watershed movement. A more recent case is that of Hirve Bazar, a drought-prone poverty-stricken village about 100 km from Pune. The efforts of one man Popatrao Pawar have converted this village into a model village. Why is it then that the Government is busy even, after 25 years, to issue guidelines—not by one ministry but by three ministries? There is a 'commitment deficit' on the part of both policy-makers and development administration.

Overall, in our over-zealous attempt to woo foreign capital, we have ignored our own saving rate. We have merrily allowed definancialisation of savings. Watershed development, a project that is so critical to future agricultural growth, has been allowed to wither away. Should we not put our priorities right?

13

A Manual for Alleviating Poverty

IT is now accepted that development economics is a failed God. This is true both in terms of theoretical constructs and policy inputs. It now transpires that efforts by economists like Robert Solow to capture the essentials of growth in a mathematical or econometric formula were misdirected. Today the World Bank's (WB) Commission on Growth and Development asserts that there is no generic formula for growth. Secondly, a recent critical appraisal of the much touted WB's *World Development Reports* (WDRs) has demonstrated that these were empty vessels offering little meaningful inputs for development policy formulation. Where do we go from here?

Writing in *Tribune* about Duncan Green's monumental volume *From Poverty to Power*, Andrew Dodgshan explains "Duncan Green Uses numerous case studies to demonstrate this book is not merely an academic textbook but a manual for real, practical and lasting social change" (revised and enlarged edition published in 2012). Duncan Green has been in the business of international development for 30 years. He was Head of Research in Oxfam for eight years. The book explores many ways in which poverty is being fought through the empowerment of people whose deprivations relate ultimately to their helplessness. The book discusses a number of different types of initiatives across the world that have enhanced and expanded powers of the powerless. There are case studies from diverse backgrounds: Brazil, Bolivia, Philippines, Israel, Egypt, China, Gautemala, Papua, New Guinea and so on. Distilling these experiences, the author has attempted to prepare a manual for alleviation of poverty.

First, the road to alleviation of poverty or development more generally, lies through the state. History has amply demonstrated that no country has prospered without active state intervention and participation. Effective state is a pre-requisite. "By effective states, we mean states that can guarantee security and the rule of law, and can design and implement an effective strategy to ensure inclusive economic growth. Effective states often known as "development states" must be accountable to citizens and able to guarantee their rights."

Secondly, state is not the only instrument for tackling poverty. What the book calls 'active citizenship' can be another effective way of seeking and securing solutions for the pervasive problem of poverty "By active citizenship we mean that combination of rights and obligations that link individuals to the state, including paying taxes, obeying laws and exercising the full range of political, civil and social rights. Active citizens use these rights to improve the quality of political or civil life, through involvement in the formal economy or formal politics or through the sort of collective action that historically has allowed poor and excluded groups to make their voices heard."

Most development practitioners now acknowledge the centrality of citizenship and the state to alleviation of poverty. This also brings into focus the need to grapple with the critical role of politics in development. This takes us to the third point namely a 'social contract'—a deal whether explicit or implicit that builds confidence and trust between citizens and the state. Finally, the book recognises the case for including private sector as a third pillar in the structure, along with the state and citizens. This is because it drives economic growth by creating jobs, transferring knowledge and technology.

Oxfam's experience on the ground suggests that some such combination of the three factors mentioned above lies at the heart of attempts to build a humane and sustainable development path-tackling inequality and poverty during the course of the current century.

While Oxfam's efforts to channel the moral outrage that global poverty evokes into effective action based on solid case studies, are welcome, it is necessary to pose the question. To what extent have we succeeded?

The dimensions of global inequality are formidable. The income of the world's 500 richest billionaires exceeds that of its poorest 416 million people. Every three minutes somewhere in the developing world, two women die needlessly in childbirth or pregnancy: Over 40 children are killed by avoidable diseases like diarrhea or malaria. Is there enough moral repugnance at the world's yawning social and economic divides? A system that allows 850 million people to go hungry, while an epidemic of obesity caused by over-feeding blights millions of lives in rich countries, is sick.

Poverty thus is not merely an economic disease, but a moral, ethical and social disease. Amartya Sen who has written a Foreword to this book quotes with approval Bernard Shaw: "The greatest of evils and the worst of crimes is poverty." Nearer home Mahatma Gandhi has given us a more graphic spectre of what poverty is about. Bhiku Parekh has admirably encapsuled the poverty profile as sketched by the Mahatma in the following paragraph:

> ...Poverty dehumanises human beings, wastes the potential and deprives their lives of all sense of meaning and purpose. It is one of the worst violence that human beings can commit against other human beings. It is as bad as killing, and even worse for the fact that it is silent, slow and invisible, and arouses no anger and is outside the purview of anyone's direct responsibility. As long as even one person is starved, is malnourished, or lacks decent housing, the social order stands indicted, lacking legitimacy. Basic human needs have the first claim on society's resources and it is an obligation to arrange its economic affairs in a manner that the needs of all members are met.

Are we heeding to the advice of the Mahatma? Not at all. Despite all the euphoria about the Indian economy being in the high growth trajectory in recent years, India continues to be the abode of the largest number of underfed and undernourished people in the world. Indian policy makers's insensitiveness to this situation was reflected in the fact that India exported a huge quantity of 27 million tonnes of rice and wheat during the three consecutive years 2001-02 to 2003-04. The same policy-makers who cut down subsidy on domestic consumption of foodgrains had no qualms about subsidising exports of rice and wheat. I had occasion to write: "If the Mahatma were alive today, he would have conducted a mass satyagraha against such thoughtless policy of exports of foodgrains". Active citizenship could perhaps have helped. Or take the recent case of mid-day meal scheme being sabotaged in Maharashtra. The unholy alliance between unscrupulous contractors and bureaucrats resulted in the supply of sub-standard food to school children. But where is the outrage?

The answer is simple. We have not inculcated the appropriate values into our society.

14

Strong Link between Financial Inclusion and Stability

THE Financial Stability and Development Council (FSDC) continues to provide, since June 2011, focused attention to potential risks to financial stability, including risks from a potential downgrade of the country's rating: the concerns arising from the elevated demand for gold and the external sector vulnerabilities of the country. The *Financial Stability Report*, the sixth in the series, was released by the Reserve Bank of India (RBI) in December 2012. The report has some unique features in the sense of going beyond the conventional confines of stability reports to raise broader issues and it may be useful to highlight them briefly at the outset. First, the strong link between financial stability and financial inclusion. In his foreword to the report, RBI Governor Dr D. Subbarao emphasises: "Over the past 60 years, we have seen several episodes of economic growth in different parts of the world. One clear lesson of this experience is that growth is sustainable only if it is inclusive. Governments around the world are therefore anxious that even as they pursue economic growth, they must make that growth process inclusive. There are many ways of understanding inclusive growth: the way I understand it is that inclusive growth is a process where the poor contribute to growth and the poor benefit from growth. A growth process that increases inequality lacks durability and even legitimacy, eventually threatening economic and social stability." That is how Dr Subbarao adds to the discourse on financial inclusion by providing a formidable rationale for financial inclusion.

The second analytical point on which Dr Subbarao throws light is the relationship between bank credit and growth. He quotes from a paper by Cecchetti and Kharoubi: "We estimate that for private credit extended by banks, the turning point is closer to 90 per cent of GDP: somewhat lower than for total credit. Many countries are closer to or beyond this level, suggesting that more credit will not translate into higher trend growth. For example, in Portugal, private credit by banks was 160 per cent of GDP at the onset of the financial crisis. The corresponding figure for UK was 180 per cent and even reached 200 per cent of GDP in Denmark. By contrast, a country like India, where bank credit is less than 50 per cent of GDP can still reap benefits from further financial deepening in terms of increasing productivity growth." In other words, there is a threshold of financial deepening beyond which further injection of credit would be counter-productive. It may lead to casino banking. The dangers of over-financialisation of the real economy have to be guarded against. More, is not, in this case, merrier.

Let us turn now to the main theme of the report, namely financial stability. For Emerging and Developing Economies (EDEs) the external environment is hostile, with the outlook for global growth continuing to be grim, the outlook for global trade depressed and capital flows are volatile. Much of the Euro area and Japan are experiencing negative growth, while growth in the US continues to be low. Although the US fiscal cliff crisis is averted for now, the Euro Area Sovereign Debt crisis is a major downside risk to global growth and financial stability. The domestic situation in India is not encouraging either. The overall macroeconomic risks in the Indian financial system have increased since the publication of the previous *Financial Stability Report* in June 2012. The twin deficits are staring at us: fiscal deficit and the current account deficit (CAD). Fiscal deficit may exceed the target of 5.4 per cent of the GDP. The current account deficit, although tending to decline, still remains high, at around 4 per cent—much above the comfort level of 2 per cent. Gold imports continue to account for a large part of the CAD. Volatile capital flows could make the CAD financing a challenge. There is a fall in domestic savings, particularly household financial savings and inflation continues to be stubbornly high. Consumer inflation continues to be in double digits.

What is however reassuring is that the Systemic Risk Survey conducted in October 2012 indicated that participants in the survey had high confidence in the stability of the Indian financial system. Indian banks are well-regulated. The Indian banking system has several inherent strengths, the most important being that banks are well capitalised both in terms of quantity and quality of capital. Profitability has been sustained. Despite these strengths, the system faces some problems. A slowing economy has raised the extent of delinquencies, with the quality of assets witnessing some deterioration. Gross non-performing advances ratio for all banks rose sharply, from 2.9 per cent at end March 2012 to 3.6 per cent at end September 2012. The report's summing up is comforting: "However, the resilience of the banking system to credit, interest rate, equality and foreign exchange shocks remains satisfactory." Macro stress test of sectoral credit risk revealed that among the selected seven sectors, agriculture is expected to register the highest NPA at 5.8 per cent by March 2013, followed by engineering, iron and steel, and construction. The adverse macroeconomic shocks have had maximum impact on engineering and iron and steel.

The implementation of Basel III Capital requirements for banks has begun on January 1, 2013, and would be completed by March 2018. Quick estimates place the additional capital requirements at ₹ 5 trillion, of which non-equity capital will be ₹ 3.25 trillion, while equity capital will be ₹ 1.75 trillion. Inclusive growth is an essential pre-requisite for any kind of stability, whether economic, political or social. Inclusive growth is largely driven by financial inclusion and an inclusive financial system. India has adopted a bank-led model for financial inclusion and in the initial stages, it was natural that the emphasis was on the physical reach of banks. The initial goal of providing access to banking services in all villages with a population of more than 2,000 by March 2012 has been successfully achieved and the focus is now on covering the remaining areas. But physical reach is only the beginning of the process of inclusion. It is the merit of this report that it gives a qualitative content to the concept of financial inclusion. The focus should now be on the volume of transactions in the newly opened accounts.

Inclusion should not be reduced to tokenism. Banks have been advised to offer a minimum of four basic products to customers:

a basic savings bank deposit account, with emergency credit facility like overdraft; a remittance product for Electronic Benefit Transfer; a savings product like a recurring deposit and a facility of entrepreneurial credit, such as General Credit Card or Kisan Credit Card. The RBI has constituted a high level Financial Inclusion Advisory Committee to strengthen the financial inclusion agenda. RBI has shown remarkable insight into issues of the under-financialisation and over-financialisation: it can surely evolve a viable and sustainable banking services delivery model which would ensure that financial inclusion and financial stability move in tandem.

II

Monetary Policy

15

Reserve Bank of India: Years of Glory

IT is not often that a journal of international repute like *The Economist*, London, showers praise on the Central Bank of a former British Colony. Sample this: "Judging by the numbers, RBI is among the world's best central banks. Its record on banking growth and inflation is decent enough. Since 1995 wholesale prices have risen by an average of 6 per cent a year, not too far from RBI's comfort zone of 5 per cent. Growth has averaged 7 per cent a year."

The journal also gives credit to the Reserve Bank of India (RBI) for escaping the Asian currency crisis of 1997 and the more recent global financial crisis of 2008.

Elaborating on the other strengths of RBI, *The Economist* emphasises: "Relative to most Indian state bodies, the RBI has more brains, muscle and integrity it is about the only institution in the country you never hear accused of graft."

The Asian currency crisis of 1997 has an interesting story behind it. RBI resisted the pressure of the International Monetary Fund (IMF) to move towards full convertibility of the rupee and that saved India. Wisdom dawned on the IMF subsequently and today IMF champions some controls on convertibility on capital account.

In the global financial crisis of 2008, when the icons of American and European financial system—commercial banks, investment banks, mortgage houses and insurance giants—collapsed like a pack of cards, the Indian financial system stood rock-like unscathed. There were two reasons for the stability of the Indian system. First, the regulatory framework was in place. The dominance of the public sector segment of the financial sector reinforced the discipline. Second, as Professor Joseph Stiglitz, the Nobel Laureate, in an interview to an Indian TV channel said: "The US financial system collapsed because we did not have a Reddy at the helm." The reference here is to Dr Y.V.

Reddy, former Governor of Reserve Bank of India, and there cannot be a better tribute to the management of the Indian financial system. Dr Reddy who was accused of being 'intolerant towards innovation', hastened slowly in introducing structured credit products. However, those Indian financial wizards who scoffed at Dr Reddy's soft-pedaling structured credit products have remained to pray.

The Economist also gives credit to RBI for retaining its multiple objectives. It may be recalled that solely inflation targeting became fashionable because it worked well for some extended period in countries like Canada, New Zealand and Thailand. Even in India some experts like Dr S.S. Tarapore, former Deputy Governor, began to advocate its adoption by RBI. The global financial crisis has demonstrated that the assumption that price stability ensures financial stability is wrong. The crisis has proved that price inflation targeting alone is inadvisable and that the mandate of Central Banks should extend beyond price stability to include bank regulation and supervision, promoting growth. RBI's multiple objectives approach stands vindicated.

In fact, it is the founding fathers of RBI who had the vision to build the promotion of rural credit into the statutes of RBI—an annual objective in the 1930s. Growth, employment and equity are among the other objectives. The nationalisation of commercial banks in 1969 has also to be viewed against this background. The branch expansion programme in the post-nationalisation period was unprecedented in the history of world banking. Much before 'financial inclusion' became fashionable, RBI had set the stage for the phenomenon.

In the initial flush of enthusiasm of implementing financial sector reforms in the early 1990s, Indian policy-makers were intoxicated with the market theology of IMF and the World Bank (WB) and hence committed major mistakes. Three of them may be highlighted here. First, the inequitable interest rate structure. Blindly adopting Basel norms, they ushered in a rate structure designed to pamper the private corporate sector and which was biased against agricultural and the small borrowers generally. For instance, a small farmer was made to pay an interest rate of 12 per cent at a time when a highly rated corporate could raise money from banks at 6 per cent. Later,

RBI admitted that this led to cross-subsidisation of economically well-off borrowers by poor borrowers. It took nearly two decades for the RBI to correct the distortion. Second, directed credit is bad and hence credit to priority sectors suffered. Banks openly defaulted on the target for priority sectors and RBI winked at the default. Third, the unkindest cut of the Basel bank culture induced by-product was the disenfranchisement of small farmers. Public sector banks were trying to boost their profits by economies of exclusion. There was a dramatic decline in the number of small borrower accounts with credit limits of ₹ 25,000. Their number, which had soared to 62.55 million in March 1992, dipped to only 36.87 million in March 2003.

Taken together, these reflect the muddying of policy waters by the contemporary Indian policy makers who were obsessed with mimicking American or British banking models, or the so-called 'international best practices.' This muddled thinking did a lot of harm to the economy. Fortunately, sanity dawned on RBI and today its *Report on Currency and Finance 2010-11* preaches: "think global, but act local." In fact it is this *mantra* which has made what is RBI today, from the founding fathers' days to Dr Reddy's days.

The Economist does not seem to have given up its market theology, unfortunately. It quotes Raghuram Rajan's view that RBI is inhibiting India's potential, India runs a 'repressed financial system,' and so on. *The Economist* must remind itself that this view is dated and that after the global financial crisis of 2008, the rationale for privatisation has all but vanished.

Finally, *The Economist's* warning: "Indeed, the thing that endangers India today is not its financial markets but its Government". The reference here is to India's fiscal deficit which may soar to 6 per cent of the GDP in 2010-11—a disturbing development. Is this deterioration in deficit just a product of financial indiscipline and 'populist politics'? In this contexts, *The Economist* quotes the present Governor Dr Subbarao: "In the presence of large sovereign borrowing ... Central Banks typically have little chance".

Another by-product of this issue is, pre-emption of banking sectors resources for Government through the prescription of Statutory Liquidity Ratio (SLR). At present SLR stands at 24 per cent. We can sympathise with *The Economist's* inability to appreciate the significance of such pre-emption because even IMF despite its continuous contact with Indian monetary authorities is unable to do so.

First, the budgetary support to our five-year development plans. Secondly, subsidies. In a society where there is no general social security, food subsidy becomes important. After the global financial crisis of 2008, economists from America or England cannot claim that markets allocate resources more efficiently. While there are no two opinions on reining in the large fiscal deficit, the manner in which it should be done should be different. Fiscal inequity should be removed: dividends received by individuals are at present totally exempt from income tax without any limit.

On the whole, *The Economist's* objective appraisal of RBI's performance in the recent period by highlighting its years of glory is indeed welcome.

16

Decimating Reserve Bank of India

IT was in March 2012 that *The Economist*, London, showered praise on Reserve Bank of India (RBI), "Judging by the numbers, RBI is among the world's best central banks. Its record on banking growth and inflation is decent enough".

The journal also gave credit to RBI for escaping Asian currency crisis of 1997 and the more recent global financial crisis of 2008. *The Economist* emphasised: "Relative to most Indian state bodies, the RBI has more brains, muscle and integrity. It is about the only institution in the country you never hear accused of graft".

RBI has thus made us proud and one would have thought that the Government of India would make every effort to further strengthen the institution. Alas! This does not seem to be so. On the other hand, there are efforts to cut it down to its size and to decimate it. Perhaps rulers like sycophancy and nobody accuses RBI of being docile. In fact it is its independent thinking which has raised its stature to its present heights.

RBI's independence was visibly demonstrated by Governor Subbarao on Tuesday the 30th October in his monetary policy announcement. Governor Subbarao did not yield to the pressure of the Minister of Finance to reduce interest rates. Governor kept the repo rate—the rate at which RBI lends to banks—unchanged at 8 per cent. Governor's only positive gesture was reduction in the cash reserve ratio—or CRR—which was cut by 25 basis points to 4.25 per cent, releasing liquidity of ₹ 17,500 crore to banks. This may enable some banks to reduce marginally their lending rates. The other positive gesture was the promise to cut key rates in January-March 2013—if inflationary pressures abate.

This monetary policy stance acquired the nature of 'confrontation' because the Finance Minister not only exhorted RBI publicly to move in tandem with fiscal policy but also left no option to RBI by sketching a road map of fiscal consolidation, a day before the announcement of monetary policy. Admitting that the fiscal deficit would exceed the budget target of 5.1 per cent to reach 5.3 per cent this year, the Finance Minister promised to bring down the deficit to 3 per cent by fiscal 2017. RBI remained unconvinced by mere numbers without spelling out concrete measures to rein in the deficit. The corporate lobby which had pinned its hopes on the Finance Minister's exhortation was disappointed and Sensex fell by 1.1 per cent to 18,430.

The Finance Minister had to grudgingly reconcile himself with the RBI stance by saying. "If Government has to walk alone to face the challenge of growth, well we walk alone."

RBI's message was loud and clear. Inflation has remained sticky at 7 per cent and its priority is to contain inflation at around 4 to 4.5 per cent in the medium term and 3 per cent in the long run. It would be therefore premature to reduce interest rates at this point of time.

Take another instance of Government of India trying to micromanage public sector banks (PSBs). Recently, the Secretary Department of Financial Services Shri D.K. Mittal has been issuing detailed directions to PSBs on purely operational matters like a cap on bulk deposit at 10 per cent of total deposits and so on. Both the present Governor Subbarao and the former Governor Dr Reddy have come out openly against such day-to-day interference with banks operations. The regulator that is RBI has to regulate: the majority owner in terms of corporate governance cannot dictate operationally. Operational autonomy of banks and regulators sole control should be respected.

Perhaps the recommendations of the Financial Sector Legislative Reforms Commission (FSLRC) put out in October 2012 in its Approach Paper may prove to be the last straw on back of RBI. It may be recalled that the FSLRC was set up in March 2011 with the mandate to evolve the new regulatory architecture for the financial sector as a whole. The Commission's final report is expected to be ready in March 2013 but the Approach Paper now released is an interim document which has invited feedback as part of the consultative process.

The Approach Paper needs to be evaluated against the present state of financial regulators-Government relationship. In India, a large number of regulators are Government owned, and there is need to introduce an element of independent regulators and also some element of autonomy. Here we restrict our comments to only those recommendations which affect RBI. One conspicuous feature of FSLRC's body of recommendations is that its hostility to RBI and its unconcealed efforts to strip RBI of most important functions which it is performing today. This is unfortunate because over the years RBI has accumulated its skills in the supervision of the different segments of the financial sector and actually nourished them. The status and shape of today's India's financial sector owes a great deal to RBI and members of FSLRC would do well to read again *The Economists* observations quoted earlier before destroying RBI—yes, this is what will result if its recommendations as spelt out in the Approach Paper are implemented. For instance, the FSLRC wants to distance RBI from the Government securities market, by setting up a separate debt management office (DMO). In the FSLRC scheme of things, the RBI will have nothing to do with forex market. What happens to exchange rate management? Or management of forex reserves of RBI? It is not possible to have an independent monetary policy in isolation of capital flows and managed exchange rate. FSLRC wants that non-banking financial companies (NBFCs) sector should be outside the purview of RBI. NBFCs do accept deposits and how could they be outside the RBI control? No where does the Approach Paper spell out the rationale for depriving RBI of these critical functions. Restricting RBI functions to monetary policy formulation and supervision of banks is neither logically sustainable nor practicable. It would serve no purpose except decimating RBI. The FSLRC would do well to revisit the whole range of issues involved.

17

The Art of Inflation Management

INFLATION continues to haunt the Indian policy makers. Food inflation for the week ended October 8 rose to 10.6 per cent from a year ago. The acceleration in food prices is lead by vegetables, fruit, milk and eggs and meat. Headline inflation has remained stubbornly high at above 9 per cent for more than a year a level way above Reserve Bank of India (RBI) comfort level of 4 or 4.5 per cent. It is not surprising that this has provoked considerable discussion both at the theoretical and policy level, on how to tame inflation.

"Inflation is one of the most dreaded and most misunderstood of economic phenomena", writes Dr Kaushik Basu, Chief Economic Adviser, Ministry of Finance, Government of India, in his scholarly article in *Economic and Political Weekly* (October 8, 2011). He takes us through a conducted tour of inflationary scenario, over time and over the globe. He emphasises that because of economists' past research and studies, today we do not have to worry about 9 per cent inflation zooming up to 30 per cent or 100 per cent or even a trillion per cent, as it happened in Hungary in 1940 or Germany in 1923. Dr Basu also discusses hyperinflation usually described as inflation over 50 per cent per month. The World's highest inflations occurred in Europe, one in 1923 and again in 1946. Comparable inflations occurred in Russia from December 1921 to January 1924, in Greece in 1943, in Zimbabwe in 2008 and in Germany in 1923. The German hyperinflation of 1923 is the most analysed and diagnosed inflation. Inflation played havoc with the economy, created political tensions that contributed to the rise of Nazism, and also caused psychological disturbances. Doctors in Germany in 1923 identified a mental illness called 'Cipher stroke' that affected many people: it referred to a neurotic urge to keep writing zeroes! The article discusses problems of using standard macroeconomic demand management tools to control inflation and the need for international coordination to control inflation in today's globalised economy. Going through this erudite discourse is indeed an intellectual pleasure.

My article seeks to argue that understanding inflation at the macro level is only the beginning of the journey towards designing measures to control inflation. While this part of the discourse may be broadly described as the science of inflation, there is also the art of controlling inflation devisiting country specific and situation specific anti-inflationary measures. Both the science and art of controlling inflation are equally important and should be mutually supportive. The art of inflation management extends beyond text book punditry.

Let me illustrate this thesis with specific reference to India.

To begin with food grains market, a large part of the food grains market is insulated from open market prices. For instance, in 2008-09, a quantum of 55.5 million tonnes of rice and wheat were procured and since procurement is done at the minimum support price (MSP), producers of rice and wheat are outside the purview of open market prices of rice and wheat. The other side of the coin is off-take of food grains from the pool of procured food grains. In 2008-09, nearly 40 million tonnes were distributed through the public distribution system (PDS). Since such distribution takes place at prescribed issue prices consumers of these food grains remain outside the purview of food grains. In this context, what is the role of the much acclaimed market signals? Look at Dr Basu's argument: "These price movements are the market's way of signaling to consumers that they should consume less of the commodity in short supply and more of the goods available in plenty, and to producers to produce more of what is in short supply, and less of what is abundant." In the Indian context the supply of agricultural commodities is rigid and not exactly responsive to price incentives.

Historically, private trade in food grains has not covered itself in glory. Traders would ensure that prices of food grains would be depressed in the post-harvest period and raised in the lean season. In this game, both the producers and the consumers were the losers and traders the gainers. With the emergence of the Food Corporation of India (FCI) as a counter-veiling force, this sort of seasonal variations in food grains has been corrected. The amplitude of seasonal variations has been moderated in favour of both the producers and consumers. What role could market signals play in this context?

Another characteristic feature of trade in agricultural commodities in India is creating artificial scarcity by hoarding of commodities by traders. That is why we have anti-hoarding laws in different states and selective credit controls so that bank finance is not used to hoard commodities.

In fact we have not fully exploited the power of the FCI which could influence the open market prices of rice and wheat by unloading appropriate quantum of its stocks in the market. Instead, we are treating FCI merely as a glorified godown keeper. Is it because we do not want to cut the profit margins of private traders in food grains?

Food inflation has been our greatest worry. Rise in prices of vegetables and fruits, milk and eggs has contributed to food inflation. Here the problem is somewhat different. Exploiting the scarcity environment traders have raised their margins appropriating a larger slice of the consumer rupee. If onions are sold at ₹ 15 per kg in Aurangabad, why should they be priced at ₹ 50 in Mumbai? Here it is a question of streamlining marketing arrangements. The Anand dairy model needs to be replicated by linking producer farmers to retail trade. Why should we wait for Walmarts to undertake this function?

The main point to drive home is that in the management of inflation, the macro level understanding through the usual money-output-prices formula or supply-demand equations may only provide the broader background: it does not provide insights to concrete policy formulation. That is where the art of inflation management becomes critical. First of all we should take a disaggregated view of inflation. Our focus should be on controlling inflation of essential commodities, especially food inflation. Here again, we should approach the segment specific issues: it may be marketing problem or a credit problem. Apart from the long-term structural problems causing supply rigidities, the art of inflation management should concentrate on immediate issues. Any discourse on inflation management remains incomplete if it does not cover these issues in the art of inflation management.

18

Micro Management of Food Inflation

INFLATION is clearly the dominant concern stated Dr D. Subbarao, Governor, Reserve Bank of India (RBI), presenting the Monetary Policy Review for 2010-11, on January 25, 2011. RBI has raised its projection of wholesale price inflation for March 2011, from its earlier level of 5.5 per cent to 7 per cent.

What is more worrying is food inflation. "The rise in food inflation has not only persisted for more than two years now; the increase has been rather sharp in the recent period" explains Governor Subbarao. It is interesting to note that the humble onions and brinjals have found a place in the lofty monetary discourse of Governor Subbarao. "Year-on-year primary food articles inflation spiked to 13.5 per cent in December from 9.4 per cent in November due to severe supply constraints in respect of some food items. In particular, vegetable prices increased by 22.9 per cent in December 2010, over the previous month's level. Month-on-month price increases were very high for some vegetables such as brinjals (65%), onions (35%), garlic (26%), cabbage (22%), tomatoes (19%) and potatoes (10%).

The price of onions which has become the most visible face of food inflation soared to ₹ 100 per kg. The earlier predictions of official *pundits* that prices of food articles would ease in December 2010 proved to be wrong. The index of food articles for the week ended January 15, 2011 was higher by 15.57 per cent than a year ago. This reversed the earlier trend of easing of prices for two consecutive weeks. The authorities seem to throw up their hands in sheer exasperation to say: "We have no instruments to control inflation!"

The food-prices crises is not a new phenomenon. A substantial rise in food prices contributes to a rise in consumer prices and thereby to inflation in general. A new term "Agflation" has been coined to describe this phenomenon of food prices fuelling inflation. The world witnessed such crisis in 2008, when higher food prices led to violent unrest across parts of the developing world.

This article seeks to argue that we have adequate number of instruments and institutions to control inflation, India's track record of containing inflation, particularly food inflation, even in more critical times like chronic shortages is excellent. We should draw upon this empirical experience, rather than bemoan the lack of instruments. What we need is micro management of food inflation. We should take a disaggregated view of the food market—commodity-wise or area-wise prices—and tackle the problem. Trade in essential articles, or food articles represents the face of predatory capitalism and this needs to be countered by creating counter-veiling forces. State intervention and activism in food market is imperative. The trouble with our contemporary policy makers, soaked as they are in the market theology of IMF and WB, is that they seem to have total trust in the invisible hand of Adam Smith to achieve the so-called 'price discovery'. Recent events, discussed above, have proved that this will not do.

First, the macro aspect. Inflation is defined, in simple terms, as too much money following too few goods. The logical policy prescription would be to contain money supply to bring down prices: this can be done through either squeezing bank credit directly or raising lending rates so that the cost of credit would lead to lower demand for credit. Obviously the money-output-price formula does not apply to the current situation. We cannot bring down the price of onions by reducing money supply.

This brings us to micro management which involves building up of market intelligence, active intervention in the market by public sector agencies and anticipatory policy responses by state and central governments. Let me illustrate.

Historically, the track record of private trade in foodgrains does not cover itself in glory. When foodgrains trade was the exclusive domain of private trade what used to happen was prices were depressed in the immediate post-harvest period while they rose significantly in the lean period. The bulk of small farmers with little holding power were compelled to sell the produce at these depressed un-remunerative prices. The consumers had to pay high foodgrains prices in the lean season. Thus both producers and consumers were the losers and the trader was the gainer. It was only with the emergence of the Food Corporation of India (FCI), as the counter-veiling power in foodgrains trade, that the amplitude of seasonal variations in foodgrains prices was substantially reduced. So far so good. With the stocks of rice and wheat being so comfortable even during this year, it should be possible for FCI to moderate the open market prices of rice and wheat by appropriate market intervention. But what is the reality? We are treating the FCI as a glorified godown keeper. Instead, we should use it as an effective mechanism to moderate the prices of rice and wheat even in the open market. FCI should become a vibrant institution armed with market intelligence to intervene in specific markets by say, unloading sizeable quantities of rice or wheat. What prevents FCI from doing this job?

About price signals. Today, we seem to think that releasing the wholesale price data on every Thursday is the be-all and end-all of price intelligence. In fact some authority at the centre should keep a continuous vigil on these data and use them as price signals for anticipatory policy formulation. We need not wait for onions prices to reach ₹ 100 before placing import orders from Pakistan or China. Anticipatory action could have saved the Government from embarrassment.

There is so much lobbying for allowing foreign direct investment (FDI) in retail trade. Why have we not streamlined our marketing channels for agricultural produce, so that the farmer's share in the consumer rupee is raised. Surely, we do not need foreign technical advice to achieve this objective. We must set our priorities right.

Again, futures trading in agricultural commodities. We seem to be swept away by textbook market theology with an inadequate understanding of the underlying processes of futures trading and its broader implications for macroeconomic management of the agricultural economy. The quantum of financial resources which are involved in futures trading is said to be astronomical. Has this phenomenon given an artificial boost to price expectations? There is very little evidence to show that the average farmer has benefited from these markets. We need to take a second look at what purposes these institutions have served.

Finally, over conventional weapons against hoarding of agricultural commodities are: state governments monitoring hoarding, and RBI not allowing bank finance to support hoarding. These need to be activated.

Although prices of vegetables and fruits will tend to ease in the next few weeks, we should not forgot this ugly episode. Rather, we should take the opportunity to build up market signals so that anticipatory policy responses could be formulated.

19

The Spectre of Inflation

THE spectre of inflation hovers over the Indian economy based on cross-country and domestic experience. The Reserve Bank of India (RBI) is strongly of the view that controlling inflation is imperative to sustaining growth over the medium-term. This is a critical attribute of a favourable investment climate, on which growth sustainability depends stated Dr Subbarao, Governor RBI, on the occasion of announcing Monetary Policy for 2011-12, on May 3, 2011.

The RBI's forecasts systematically under-predicted year-end inflation during 2010-11. Even after a sizeable upward revision from 5.5 per cent to 7 per cent in January 2011, and then to 8 per cent in March 2011, the forecasts remained below the actual level of 9 per cent for March 2011. The analysis provided in the policy documents reveals that the surge in headline inflation was the combination of two factors, an unanticipated increase in oil and commodity prices. The stance of monetary policy in 2011-12 will be therefore to contain perceptions of inflation in the range of 4 to 4.5 per cent.

With this objective in mind, Dr Subbarao announced a package of measures to tighten the monetary situation. The more important of these measures were: (i) the repo rate—that is the rate at which banks borrow from RBI has been raised by 50 basis points from 6.75 per cent to 7.25 per cent and (ii) the interest rate on saving banks deposits has been raised from 3.5 per cent to 4 per cent. Although savings banks deposits constitute only about 22 per cent of total deposits for the banking system, nonetheless this will raise the cost of funds to banks and banks are expected to raise their lending rates, as a consequence.

While the first measure is a monetary tightening measure, the second is designed to correct a historical distortion. The interest rate on savings has remained unchanged for the last 8 years although rates on other deposits have been adjusted upwards. This is unfair to the small saver, who needs to be given an incentive.

As expected commercial banks raised their lending rates by 80 basis points on May 4. IDBI bank was the first to raise and others like Punjab National Bank (PNB), Oriental Bank of Commerce (OBC) and Yes Bank followed.

Actually, RBI measures were a mild dose of anti-inflationary medicine. For instance, their was no increase in the bank rate which remained at 6 per cent. Nor was there any increase in the cash reserve ratio (CRR) of commercial banks, which remained unchanged at 6 per cent of net demand and time liabilities (NDTL). If RBI really wanted to squeeze liquidity in the system and raise the cost of funds both these rates would have been raised. But the Indian corporate body is quite sensitive to even marginal rise in interest rates. The capital market reacted sharply. The apprehension was that higher lending rates would dent corporate earnings. The Sensex dropped by 463 points or 2.4 per cent to touch 18,534 on May 4. This easy trend continued and there was another sharp decline of 259 points on May 5, the index touching 18,211. The Indian corporate sector's sensitiveness even to marginal increase in lending rates is thus clear.

In any case, RBI's baseline projection for wholesal price index (WPI) inflation for March 2012 is projected at 6 per cent with an upward bias.

Contrast this RBI approach to corporate sector lending rates with the lending rates for the small borrower particularly in the rural sector. The Malegam Committee of RBI has endorsed the proposal that the microfinance institutions (MFIs) can charge the small borrowers an interest rate of 26 per cent. It is alright for private MFIs to charge such usurious rates but that the Central Bank of the country should lend respectability to such rates is beyond all economic logic.

While discussing about control of inflation, we should remember that in India inflation is not a purely monetary phenomenon. These measures on the monetary front need to be buttressed by measures in the real sector. For instance, we have ample stocks of rice and wheat with the Food Corporation of India (FCI)—stocks which are far in excess of buffer stocks norms. We should plan to influence open market prices of rice and wheat by unloading appropriate quantities of rice and wheat in the open market. The record of FCI in this field is poor.

In recent months, the prices of fruits and vegetables played havoc contributing greatly to food inflation. If onions are sold at ₹ 15 per kg in Aurangabad, why should they be priced at ₹ 50 in Mumbai? Here it is a question of streamlining the marketing arrangements to enable the producer-farmer to get a fair share in the consumer rupee. The milk marketing pattern of Anand offers a good model. Both the state and Central Governments should strive to organise such cooperatives for producers of fruits and vegetables.

20

In the Aftermath of Monetary Tightening

PRIVATE corporate sector seems to be up in arms against Reserve Bank of India (RBI). Governor Dr Subbarao announced on July 26, as part of the First Quarter Review of Monetary Policy for 2011-12: raising of the repo rate at which RBI lends to banks by 50 basis points to 8 per cent. Also, the Reverse Repo rate, the rate RBI pays to banks for their investment of their surplus funds with it, was raised to 7 per cent. The point is that this move by RBI signals banks to raise their lending rates. This is what worries the corporate sector which was expecting only a quarter per cent rise the now famous baby steps of Dr Subbarao. RBI's adult step has 'shocked' some corporate spokesman who have argued that this will 'hurt', if not 'kill', growth. Indeed the expected outcome manifested itself within hours of RBI's announcement: Yes Bank, a private sector bank, raised its base rate by 50 basis points to 10.25 per cent. Other banks are expected to follow.

The capital market reflected this corporate sentiment. The Sensex declined for three consecutive days, on 26th by 353 points to 18,518; and further to 18,432 on 27th and to 18209 on 28th. The question to pose is: Is a half-percentage point rise in repo rate so damaging to the economy? This article seeks to argue that the apprehensions of the corporate sector are highly exaggerated and that control of inflation is in the long-term interest of the corporate sector itself.

First, about inflation. In terms of macroeconomics inflation continues to be the dominant concern. The headline inflation measured by wholesale price index (WPI) for the first quarter of 2011-12 remained stubbornly above 9 per cent, almost close to double digits. Inflation pressures have also continued to remain broad-based. This has happened despite the measures taken by RBI recently. Since October 2009, which marked the 'exit' policy of RBI from its crisis driven expansionary regime, RBI raised the cash reserve ratio (CRR) by 100 basis points and also the repo rate 10 times by a cumulative 275 basis points. This has made imperative that RBI should pursue its anti-inflationary policy with greater vigour. RBI's rationale is summed up as follows: "However, considering the persistence of inflation above the comfort level of the Reserve Bank, and based on the premise that high inflation is inimical to long-term growth, the Reserve Bank has persevered with its anti-inflationary stance in 2011-12."

The broader philosophy underlying the anti-inflationary stance was spelt out by RBI in the May 2011. Policy statement: "Reserve Bank is strongly of the view that controlling inflation is imperative both for sustaining growth over the medium-term and for increasing the potential growth rate. This is a critical attribute of a favourable investment climate on which the economy's potential growth depends."

There is yet another reason why RBI has to become more aggressive. Dr Subbarao has put it politely "... in the absence of complimentary policy responses on both demand and supply sides, stronger monetary policy actions are required. Government of India has budgeted a fiscal deficit of 4.6 per cent of GDP for 2011-12. Subsequent developments like larger subsidy burden have made the meeting of the target rather difficult. Larger fiscal deficit has thus been a major source of demand pressures."

Thus creating a stable price regime would itself help corporate growth.

There are other extenuating factors for the corporate sector. The buoyancy in exports has continued. Export growth in the first quarter of 2011-12 was 46 per cent over the corresponding quarter of the previous year. This should act as a booster to corporate growth. The resilience in export performance has resulted from the supportive government policy, focusing on the diversification in terms of higher value-added products in engineering and petroleum sectors and destinations across developing economies.

The outlook for 2011-12 continues to be rosy. The south-west monsoon has been so far only one per cent below normal. The forecast for GDP growth in 2011-12 is retained at 8 per cent, as against the growth of 8.5 per cent in 2010-11.

The conclusion that emerges from this brief discussion is that even if there is an increase in lending rates of banks by one per cent, this is not going to hurt growth. First, interest cost is only about 5 per cent of total cost and hence the resultant increase in cost to the industry would be nominal. Second, the corporate earnings are healthy and could easily provide the necessary cushion for absorbing the rise in cost. All the sound and fary that the corporate sector, has made is unwarranted. RBI's interest rate regime in the past has pampered the corporate sector. For instance, in the Prime Benchmark interest rate regime, small borrowers subsidised large borrowers. Fortunately, this distortion stands corrected now under the base rate regime. But the corporate sector is quite vocal and hence makes appropriate noises to protect its privileges.

How does a rise in lending rates help in moderating inflation? Corporate borrowers would rationalise their bank borrowings in response to the higher cost of bank credit. This would moderate the demand for bank credit. For instance, the projection for non-food bank credit growth has been revised downwards from the earlier level of 19 per cent to 18 per cent. This has implications for money supply expansion. The projected figure of 16 per cent growth in broad money (M3) has been revised downwards to 15.5 per cent. This is how inflation is sought to be tamed through deceleration in bank credit and money supply growth.

When inflation continued to remain above the comfort level that is above the RBI's projected levels, there was a strong case for a big-bank approach. A significant rise in the reserve ratio, for instance, conveys RBI's message in clear and loud terms. Baby steps are of little avail under such circumstances. Empirical experience corroborates this, approach, as RBI's policy action in the 1980s demonstrates. Such drastic steps have a demonstration effect in the sense that bankers are made to sit up and follow a more discriminatory policy of disbursing credit both quantitatively and qualitatively. One hopes that this adult step of RBI Governor would yield the desired results.

21

Monetary Policy and the Growth Syndrome

ON the eve of the monetary policy announcement on the June 18, the Indian economy appeared to be on the throes of a crisis. In the January-March 2012 quarter, GDP growth slumped to 5.3 per cent—the lowest during the last nine years. For the year 2011-12 as a whole growth works out to 6.5 per cent, lower than the projected level. The rupee-dollar rate dropped to ₹ 57 per US dollar, recording a 20 per cent depreciation over the year. India's attractiveness as an investment destination has taken a beating, with inflow of foreign investment reduced to a trickle. This state of the Indian economy has to be viewed in the broader context of the global environment which is likely to have an adverse impact on growth and inflation in developing economies, particularly on oil importing countries like India.

Against such a depressing background, there was enormous pressure on the Reserve Bank of India (RBI) to reduce its policy rates to enable banks to lower their lending rates. Cheap money promotes growth. The pressure was not only from the corporate sector which would be the greatest beneficiary of lower lending rates but also from the Ministry of Finance. The fiscal deficit of 5.6 per cent of GDP was quite embarrassing for the ministry and some monetary easing would help in deflecting the attack on the ministry for its fiscal profligacy.

It is to the credit of RBI Governor Subbarao that he successfully resisted these pressures to demonstrate that real life situations are for more complicated to be amenable to text book solutions. Monetary policy making remains an art and not a science.

RBI's penetrating analysis highlights the following three points. First, the current growth-inflation dynamics is that there are several factors, other than interest rates, responsible for the slowdown in activity, particularly investment. Public investment is shrinking at a time when reviving investment, both public and private, is a critical imperative. The widening current account deficit (CAD), despite the slowing down in growth is symptomatic of demand-supply imbalances and a pointer to the urgent need to resolve the supply bottlenecks. The persistence of inflation, both at wholesale and retail levels, is a clear indication of supply bottlenecks.

Secondly, the role of interest rates in influencing economic growth needs to be assessed afresh. The current real—adjusted for inflation—effective bank lending rates, though positive, remain comparatively lower than the levels seen during the high growth phase of 2003-2008. This demonstrates that factors other than interest rates are contributing more significantly to the growth slowdown.

Thirdly, reduction in policy interest rates at this juncture would exacerbate inflationary pressures, rather than supporting growth.

Thus the monetary policy announcement on the June 18 conveyed RBI's decision to keep the policy repo rate—the rate at which it lends to banks—unchanged at 8 per cent. Secondly, the cash reserve ratio (CRR) of banks also remained unchanged at 4.75 per cent of their net demand and time liabilities. This was a clear signal that the RBI would not enable banks to reduce their lending rates. The corporate sector's hopes thus crashed and this was reflected in the BSE Sensex declining by 244 points to 16,705.

The over-riding consideration in Governor Subbarao's mind seems to be the threat of inflation gathering further steam. During 2012-13, headline inflation as measured by wholesale price index (WPI) rose from 7.2 per cent in April to 7.6 per cent in May 2012. What is worse consumer price index (CPI) rose from 8.8 per cent in February to 9.4 per cent in March and further to 10.4 per cent in April 2012. This double digit consumer price inflation is eating into savings and pulling down the standard of living of the vast majority. Governor Subbarao put it bluntly: "Poor people are hit by inflation. Inflation is a regressive tax, hurts the poor most. Their voice, silent as it is, must also be heard." One hopes the corporate sector's frustration at the lending rates not declining, will be tempered by Governor's plain speaking.

Boosting the Economy: June 25 Measures

Another positive impact of Governor Subbarao's presentation was that Government was prodded to come up with—other than monetary policy initiatives to boost the economy. The then Finance Minister Pranab Mukherjee announced that a package of measures, jointly worked out by RBI and Government, would be unveiled soon. These measures announced on June 25 are designed to encourage flow of foreign debt: these included allowing companies with forex earnings to raise foreign borrowings upto $10 billion: increased limit for foreign institutional investors (FIIs) investment in Government debt from $15 billion to $20 billion: relaxed norms for foreign debt investment in infrastructure. Further, the indicative external commercial borrowing ceiling for 2012-13 has been increased from $30 billion to $40 billion. RBI's measures may help in bringing in larger quantum of foreign exchange. Market analysts feel these measures are not strong enough to reverse the current trend of outflow of foreign funds. The Sensex dipped by 90 points to 16,882. The corporate expected a more aggressive package and their disappointment is clear.

What Ails the Economy?

In today's global economy, deceleration of growth is a common feature of most countries and in this context a 6 per cent growth for India is good enough. Where is the crisis? The problem really is to put back the Indian economy into its normal 8 per cent growth trajectory. There is really no justification for so much of pessimism particularly of the corporate sector. Perhaps it is for the first time that corporate leaders have come out openly criticising the Government for what they call policy paralysis—not pushing reform of banking and insurance, not clearing mega projects, and not taking any policy initiatives to boost the economy. Strangely enough the prospect of change of guard at the Finance Ministry lifted the pessimism and the Sensex rose to 17,032 on June 21. Is this irrational exuberance? As if to prove the corporate leaders right, the Prime Minister is reported to have exhorted the officials: "Investor sentiment is down and capital flows are drying up... Reverse the climate of pessimism... Raise the animal spirit in the economy" (June 27). He has set himself the task of reviving the animal spirits of businessman, attracting capital inflows to prop up the rupee and revisiting aggressive tax regime. Market sentiment is an elusive entity not easily amenable to rational assessment. One hopes the Prime Minister's magic will work.

22

Monetary Policy

Drama and Realities

THE monetary policy measures, announced by Dr Subbarao, Governor, Reserve Bank of India (RBI) on 16th September had an element of drama. First, Dr Kaushik Basu, Chief Economic Advisor, had openly expressed his view that there should be a 'pause' in the process of monetary tightening. His opposition to hike in interest rates was based on the recent experience of Turkey. Despite high inflation Turkey began lowering interest rates from the middle of last year. What happened was interesting. Turkey's growth rate rose comparable to China's growth rate.

Inflation far from rising declined from 10 per cent in April 2010 to around 5 per cent. The counter argument is that Turkey lowered interest rates not so much with the objective of controlling inflation as to counter massive capital inflows. Dr Basu also cited the empirical experience of South Korea during the period 1956 to the 1970s when high growth co-existed with high inflation. Dr Basu needs to be reminded that such random examples of empirical experiences have hardly any relevance for contemporary policy making in India. As the World Bank's Growth Report has emphasised, "there is no generic formula for growth. Each country has specific characteristics and historical experiences that must be reflected in its growth strategy." This is equally relevant for controlling inflation. Inflation in India has some distinct characteristics, as we will presently explain. The point is that such open disagreement of the Ministry of Finance was an embarrassment for RBI.

The second dimension of the dramatic element was the reason of the private corporate sector, which has all along been pampered by Governments and RBI. In the September policy measures, all that happened was a hike in the policy repo rate that is the rate at which RBI lends to banks by 25 basis points from 8 per cent to 8.25 per cent.

The corporate sector's argument is that this is the 12th rate hike in the last 18 months and such aggressive monetary tightening will hurt the growth of the economy.

Dr Subbarao is dubbed as 'a man killing India's growth'. An objective analysis would show that all this is exaggerated and there is little substance in it. For instance, even a 12 times hike in interest rate translates in only a 3 per cent increase. For stubbornly high inflation a much higher increase is called for. If we look at the experience of the 1980s, we realise that such increases were implemented without much fuss. What is wrong is perhaps the so-called 'baby steps'. It would have been more appropriate to have achieved this objective by bigger steps.

The appetite of the corporate sector for cheaper loans is insatiable. Even if this 3 per cent increase in the repo rate translates itself into say 1 per cent increase in bank's lending rate it would not hurt corporate sector. Because interest cost forms only 5 per cent of total costs in any industry. All the sound and fury made by the corporate sector has thus no concrete basis.

The critical line in Dr Subbarao's statement is "Meanwhile, inflation remains high, generalized and much above the comfort zone of the Reserve Bank." Inflation as measured by head-line year-on-year wholesale price index (WPI) rose from 9.2 per cent in July to 9.8 per cent in August 2011. Food inflation which hurts the middle class and the poor most is at near-double digit levels. What is more, this sort of inflation persists despite comfortable stokes of rice and wheat, and normal monsoons. Advance estimates for the 2011-12 *kharif* season indicate a record production of rice, oilseeds, and cotton. Perhaps, this inflation is being "driven by structural demand-supply imbalances and cannot be dismissed as a temporary phenomenon."

Dr I.G. Patel, former Governor RBI, used to repeatedly emphasise that our blessed country is not exempt from basic monetary laws. Money supply (M3) growth at 18.7 per cent in August 2011 was higher than the projected growth of 15.5 per cent for the year. Similarly non-food credit growth at 20.1 per cent in August 2011 was above the indicative projection of 18 per cent for the year. The marginal increase of 25 basis points in the repo rate announced by Dr Subbarao is the minimum he could have done.

All the sound and fury generated by the measure does not signify much. The hike in the repo rate is symbolic and not substantive. Banks are unlikely to transmit the rise to borrowers. Perhaps some marginal rise in home loans or loans to real estate is possible. The corporate sector will not suffer. The question of killing growth risks to India's robust growth may arise from other sources. Dr Subbarao points out "Although India's exports have performed extremely well in the recent period, this trend is unlikely to be sustained in the face of weakening global demand."

The faltering US recovery and the Euro crisis endangered by the debt problems of Greece and other countries would affect India's exports. Fortunately, India has already diversified its exports and areas other than the US and Europe today account for a substantial proportion of India's total exports. This should save us from a serious dent in our exports.

RBI is no doubt fighting a brave battle against the stubborn inflation. But this action needs to be reinforced by measures in the real sectors. First, we must seek to bring down the open market prices of rice and wheat. Fortunately, we have enough stocks of rice and wheat with the Food Corporation of India (FCI). But unfortunately we are treating FCI as a glorified godown keeper. We should activate FCI to intervene in the market by unloading its stocks with a view to bringing down open market prices of rice and wheat. FCI should become a market maker.

Similarly, recent experience has shown that prices of other food items like vegetables and fruits have contributed significantly to rise in the prices of essential commodities. Here the problem is that the profits of intermediaries are very high, with the share of the farmer in the consumer rupee continuing to remain low. Streamlining the marketing arrangements of such commodities should receive immediate attention. We seem to be waiting for Walmarts to solve the problem of linking the farmer to the consumer, eliminating unnecessary intermediaries. But we have our own model of milk marketing in the Anand dairy. If we are able to replicate such marketing models in respect of other essential commodities, we could not only succeed in controlling food inflation but also improve levels of farm incomes. We should learn to contend with these more mundane realities.

23

Our Financial Sector Remains Stable

THERE is no standard or unique definition of financial stability. One broad definition runs along the following lines; an environment which ensures uninterrupted financial transactions, maintenance of a level of confidence in the financial system amongst all participants and stakeholders and absence of excessive volatility that unduly and adversely affects real economic activity. Financial stability is thus essential for realising sustained growth. In the wake of several financial crisis that occurred worldwide and the devastating implications of the crises to respective economies, financial stability is now recognised as a critical function of Central Banks.

The approach adopted by Reserve Bank of India (RBI) to maintain financial stability is multi-pronged: maintenance of overall macroeconomic balance through monetary policy; improvement in the macro-prudential functioning of institutions and markets; and strengthening of micro-prudential institutional soundness through regulation and supervision. RBI implemented in the 1990s financial sector reforms in a prudent and phased manner so as to ensure a smooth transition of the financial system to the best international standards and practices.

The record of RBI in term of weathering international crises is commendable: for example the East Asian crisis in 1997 or the global financial crisis of 2008.

RBIs Financial Stability Report, released in June 2011, is a scholarly document which provides a wealth of information on not only India's financial system but also global financial system: Governor Dr Subbarao assures us in his Foreword. "The Indian financial sector has remained stable. Banks are well capitalized: the Reserve Bank continues to be vigilant and has taken certain prudential as well as macro-prudential measures in order to enhance the soundness of the banking system while the focus of regulating the non-banking space continues to be on leverage and systemic inter connectedness a comprehensive review is under way to revisit certain broad principles that underpin the regulatory architecture keeping in view the economic role and heterogeneity of this sector and the recent international experience."

Institutionally, the Financial Stability Development Council (FSDC) and its Sub-Committee for monitoring financial stability on an ongoing basis have been operationalised.

In contrast, the global scenario is far from encouraging. The sovereign debt crisis in countries like Greece, Portugal and Ireland is posing serious challenges for the stability in the entire Euro area. The higher levels of Government debt in other advanced countries are adding to the uncertainty around the fiscal consolidation and its impact on international financial markets. Emerging Market Economies (EMEs) have more comfortable fiscal space and better growth prospects. The international prices of food, energy and commodities are expected to remain high during 2011-12. Inflation at the global level is a concern as persistence of high global commodity prices would result in lower growth and higher inflation dispersed all over.

Reverting to the Indian scenario, the Report not only highlights the strength of the Indian system but also its weaknesses. For commercial banks, the concerns are: increased reliance on market borrowings to fund assets, increasing imbalances in the maturity profile of assets and liabilities and potential addition to asset impairment which could follow the rebound in credit off-take.

Credit growth rebounded in 2010-11 with 22.6 per cent growth in outstanding credit after a subdued performance in the previous year. To assess the impact of credit growth on banks asset quality, an empirical study was conducted to analyse the related trends in the periods identifiable with pre-global financial crisis, its aftermath and the post-crisis phase. The study revealed that strong credit growth was synonymus with lowering of the risk perceptions leading to perceptible improvement in asset quality, whereas slowdown in credit growth was followed by increase in impaired assets. The Report therefore advocates increased caution in credit selection and stringent monitoring standards to ensure that the credit growth remained immune to potential impairments should a slow down were to take place.

Exposure to priority sectors increased but high level of NPAs (non-performing assets) was a cause of concern. Priority sector credit grew by 21 per cent in 2010-11 as against its impaired assets which increased by 28 per cent. The asset quality of exposures to the priority sector especially agriculture, continued to compare unfavourably with the overall NPA ratio of the banking sector. Consequently, the gross NPA ratio for the priority sector deteriorated from 3.3 per cent to 3.5 in 2010-11.

Regional rural banks (RRBs) have a large branch network in the rural areas of 11,861, accounting for 37 per cent of total rural branch network. RRBs are categorised into three categories sustainable viable with 55 RRBs, current viable with 24 RRBs, and loss making with 3 RRBs. An analysis of the performance of the 3 loss making and 24 other RRBs in the current viable category revealed some concerns. In order to align RRBs with the operational efficiency gained by other banks through information technology (IT) enabled products, a Road Map for adoption of Core Banking Solution (CBs) in RRBs has been finalised.

In the co-operative credit system financial soundness remained an area of concern. While the NPA ratios improved for the short-term co-operative credit institutions like State Cooperative Banks and District Central Cooperative Banks, for the long-term institutions like State Co-operative Agricultural and Rural Development Bank (SCARDB) the ratios deteriorated further. Though the norms in respect of minimum capital adequacy ratios have not been prescribed for the rural cooperative credit institutions, its disclosure has been put in place since March 2008.

In the field of Urban Cooperative Banks (UCBs) consolidation exercise continued. This has resulted in reduction in the number of weak and unlicenced banks in the sector. Consequently, financial soundness has improved.

The non-banking financial companies (NBFCs) sector posses certain important problems because of its heterogeneity and its systemic interconnectedness. There are Deposit Taking NBFCs and Non-Deposit taking NBFCs. The regulation of this sector has been progressively tightened. The capital to risk-weighted assets ratio (CRAR) of both the categories has been raised to 15 per cent from the earlier stipulation of 12 per cent. Provisioning for standard and assets and a prudential cap on banks exposures to debt oriented mutual funds have also been stipulated. A Working Group on NBFCs is examining issues related to regulatory gaps and identifying arbitrage opportunities that exist in the system, enhancing disclosure requirements and improved supervisory practices.

Some reforms have been introduced in the microfinance institutions (MFIs), following Malegam Committee recommendations: for instance, the conditionalities for considering as priority sector loans have been tightened.

Within the RBI, a number of initiatives have been taken to upgrade the financial stability analytics to appraise systemic risk. Though systemic risk management is in its early stages of evolution, here an attempt has been made to identify, monitor and address systemic linkages through network analyses model. Inter-regulatory collaboration has also become essential for financial stability. This Report includes contributions from Securities and Exchange Board of India (SEBI) and the Insurance Regulatory and Development Authority (IRDA), on systemic issues pertaining to their segments. One hopes that further research and analysis in this area will be policy-oriented so that concrete reforms could be formulated at the ground level.

24

Monetary Easing

A Heroic Step

SUBBARAO stuns with a Giant Repo Rate Cut—that is how a leading financial daily welcomed the monetary easing measure announced by RBI Governor Dr D. Subbarao on April 17, 2012, as part of the Monetary Policy statement for 2012-13. Even making allowance for the hyperbolic element in the headline, the measure represents a heroic step as this article would seek to spell out.

First, the measures. The repo rate that is the rate at which banks borrow from RBI is reduced from 8.5 per cent to 8 per cent with immediate effect. This is a signal for banks to reduce their lending rates. This measure was further buttressed by enlarging the size of liquidity cushion. The borrowing limit of scheduled commercial banks was raised under the marginal standing facility (MSF) from 1 per cent to 2 per cent of their net demand and time liabilities (NDTL):

Thus not only the cost of borrowing from RBI is reduced but also there will be ample liquidity to banks. This is sufficient inducement to banks to ease their lending rates. It may be recalled here that liquidity conditions had remained in a deficit mode throughout 2011-12. The net injection of liquidity under the Liquidity Adjustment Facility (LAF) which had peeked to ₹ 2 trillion on March 20, 2012, declined sharply to ₹ 0.7 trillion on April 13, 2012.

IDBI was the first to respond to RBI's signal: it reduced its lending and fixed deposits rates by 0.25 per cent from April 20, other public sector undertaking (PSU) banks including the Punjab National Bank and Bank of Maharashtra followed. Because of competition, private sector banks like ICICI are also expected to follow.

Without waiting for other banks to respond, the Secretary, Union Financial Services, has asked all PSU banks to have a 'relook' at all lending rates very quickly. The rate of direct lending to agriculture has to be fixed at 13.5 per cent. Fixing interest rates of public sector banks (PSBs) is the prerogative of RBI and is the Government of India eroding RBI's autonomy?

Why is this monetary easing by Dr Subbarao regarded as a heroic effort? There are two reasons. First, most macroeconomic parameters were actually warning against easing. Three such indicators may be considered: fiscal deficit, current account deficit on balance of payments, and potential threats of resurgence of inflation.

As noted in the 2012-13 Union Budget, overshooting of expenditure on subsidies was one of the main reasons for deterioration of fiscal balance in 2011-12. The gross fiscal deficit rose from 4.9 per cent of GDP in 2010-11 to 5.9 per cent in 2011-12. Although the 2012-13 budget seeks to rein in the deficit to 5.1 per cent, the task is formidable. During April-December 2011, India's current account deficit (CAD) widened to 4 per cent of GDP from 3.3 per cent in April-December 2010, largely reflecting a higher trade deficit. Consequently there was a draw down in our foreign exchange reserves to the extent of US$ 7 billion. This level of CAD is unsustainable and needs to be contained. Normally 2 per cent of CAD is regarded as a safe level.

Inflation in 2011-12 evolved broadly along the trajectory projected by RBI. The March 2012 inflation at 6.9 per cent was closer to RBI's projection of 7 per cent. The projection for inflation for March 2013 is placed at 6.5 per cent. But Dr Subbarao warns that although inflation as measured by wholesale price index (WPI) has softened, inflation as measured by the consumer price index (CPI) increased sharply from 7.7 per cent in January to 8.8 per cent in February reflecting a reversal in food inflation. Thus price pressures at the retail level continue to be a cause for concern.

Despite these adversarial conditions, why did Dr Subbarao choose to ease monetary policy after three years of monetary tightening? The reply is that growth considerations dominated over inflation containment. GDP growth during April-December 2011 slowed down substantially to 6.9 per cent from 8.1 per cent during the corresponding period of the previous year. Against this background, the change in the stance of the monetary policy reflects "an adjustment of policy rates consistent with the current growth moderation." Growth in GDP is expected to recover gradually in 2012-13, though modestly to say 7.3 per cent.

Corporate sector was quite vocal in expressing its discomfiture at continuing monetary tightening and, the consequent rise in banks lending rates. A couple of days earlier before the RBI policy announcement, the Finance Minister had already given hopes to the corporate sector about the possible monetary easing. A second reason which made Dr Subbarao's measure bold was the magnitude of reduction in the repo rate. In fact Dr Subbarao had all along preferred 'baby steps' and hence the general expectation was a reduction by 0.25 per cent. Hence the reduction by 0.50 per cent had a good demonstration effect. The sensex rose by 1.2 per cent to 17,358 on the 18th April.

In terms of immediate outcome at least Dr Subbarao's heroic step has yielded results: lending, rates have declined, though modestly and these measures have also boosted corporate confidence. Whatever the cynics may say about defying macroeconomic indicators discussed earlier, Dr Subbarao's gamble has paid off.

Fortunately, the Meteorological Department has predicted a normal monsoon this year and hence farm growth could stay close to the trend level. Industry is expected to perform better than last year and the corporate despondency has been lifted by RBI's efforts to lower lending rates. On the whole, GDP growth in 2012-13 should be above the 7 per cent level. The change in the stance of monetary policy from being focused exclusively on controlling inflation to "being sensitive to risks to growth and other vulnerabilities" would have been justified.

At the end, one general comment seems warranted. We seem to lay too much emphasis on monetary policy for macroeconomic management. Real factors are equally important. The slowdown in growth of the economy has been driven by a sharp fall in investment, some moderation in private consumption and a fall in external demand. RBI's paper on the economy also highlights the need for prudent external sector management. Why should a poor country be encouraged to import annually $50 billion worth of gold and silver? We should address these real sector issues with a sense of urgency.

25

Micro Credit and the Financial System

THE 2010 microfinance crisis in Andhra Pradesh has raised some basic questions regarding the role that microfinance institutions (MFIs) can play in future in providing access to finance to the poor. If the microfinance sector shrinks in future, what are the feasible credit alternatives we could think of for filling the gap? A recent paper by the World Bank (WB) explores the alternatives (After the Microfinance Crisis: Assessing the Role of Government-led Micro Credit Alternatives, 2011).

Can the cooperative credit institutions cope with the challenge? The WB conducted a survey in 2007 in three districts in Andhra Pradesh to assess the performance of rural credit cooperatives in particular Primary Agricultural Credit Cooperatives (PACs). The findings of this Survey are interesting. The findings also clearly reflect WB's own bias in favour of private and against Government-led or Government sponsored institutions. First, we find evidence that PACs were used as political instruments and that borrowers responded by prioritising all debt obligations (MFIs, informal lenders, etc.) before repayment of PACs loans. This indicates that the culture of repaying institutions with significant government involvement may have been low and that a private sector solution that is shielded from the Government's interference may be desirable. This is a very simplistic interpretation and it demonstrates how innocent are the WB experts about the Indian financial system.

But let us look at the deficiencies of PACs, as revealed by the survey. First Secretaries of PACs had an average of only 1.5 years of education. They had been trained in accounting for less than two months. Presidents of PACs on the other hand had higher qualifications. This led to dominance of Presidents in the governance of PACs. Admission and termination of members and credit decisions were influenced by them. Loan decisions of PACs tended to favour certain members. PACs Presidents do not look after members interests. Then there is the role of politics. For instance, agricultural credit increases by 5 to 10 percentage points in an election year.

The point is that our approach to streamline the operations of PACs should be: how to correct these deficiencies and develop PACs on healthy lines. We cannot throw away the baby along with the bath water.

What is most unfortunate is that the WB experts have not cared to view the problems in the specific context of the evolution of the Indian financial system. Otherwise they would not have made the following comment: "If an expanded role for government has to be the solutions, care should be taken in ensuring that efforts of government interventions have the intended consequences."

The WB experts seem to assume that MFIs are the ideal credit institutions to reach the poor. This is tantamount to begging the whole question. They should have cared to look at the Indian experience. The ordinance of Andhra Government is quite explicit. "Where as these SHGs are being exploited by private Micro Finance Institutions (MFIs) through usurious interest rates and coercive means of recovery resulting in their impoverishment and in some cases leading to suicides...." The engagement of MFIs with borrower was shallow based on 'touch and move on' business models, shorn of any development content. The small loan size and short duration of the loan do not enable most borrowers to do much except to ease liquidity problems. That is why Dr Y.V. Reddy former Governor, RBI, stated that microfinance is India's subprime. "Ultimately, it is something like subprime lending": In fact there is evidence to show that profit-making MFIs were encouraging what were called 'NINJA' loans—no income, no job and no assets—in the American financial crisis of 2008.

Part of the problem of WB experts is that they take a compartmentalised view of MFIs or cooperative credit institutions and are still not grown up from the now discredited market theology. Financial system has to be viewed as an integrated whole. The WB experts should have first understood the milieu in which they are discussing the role of cooperative credit institutions. The evolution of the Indian financial system is unique in a number of ways. We must pay a tribute to the vision of policy makers of the 1970s. Much before financial inclusion became fashionable internationally, these policy makers took concrete steps to usher in financial inclusion: nationalisation of major banks in 1969, the phenomenal branch expansion programme—a programme unprecedented in the history of world banking—and fixing credit targets with a view to ensure a wider disbursal of bank credit. Reaching the small borrowers and the poor thus became the objective of the whole financial system and not the exclusive preserve of profit-making MFIs. The Indian financial system is thus a product of state direction and guidance.

Again, India is unique in building up its home-grown segment of microfinance public sector banks (PSBs), restructured regional rural banks (RRBs), rejuvenated cooperative credit system, and NABARD's self-help groups (SHGs) Bank Linkage Programme (SBLP) which has emerged as a major channel of microfinance. Then, there is the post office, which already functions as a semi-bank with its 1.55 lakh branches and some 16 crore customers. This holds out great promise for emerging as a major microfinance institution. In the Indian financial milieu, therefore, there is no space for the new breed of Shylocks who masquerade as profit-making MFIs.

26

RBI's 'Honeymoon' with Microfinance

THE recent confrontation between the Reserve Bank of India (RBI) and the Andhra Pradesh Government on the regulation of microfinance institutions (MFIs) raises much broader issues than merely the legal question of turf—who should regulate the MFIs, RBI or State Governments? RBI has not covered itself in glory in its handling of MFIs. The founding fathers of RBI wanted RBI to emerge as a friend and philosopher of small borrowers generally and small farmers particularly. Till 1991 when the so-called financial sector reforms were introduced, RBI had consistently discharged its responsibilities as envisaged by the founding fathers. Alas, the reform mania prompted RBI to betray this trust in the post-reform period, as we will discuss presently. This manifested itself in the evolution of an inequitable interest rate structure, which was biased against small borrowers and favoured larger borrowers, say of the corporate sector.

We need to focus on the substantive point of Andhra Government that RBI has failed to address the core issues of MFIs. In fact Andhra Government deserves to be congratulated on its ordinance issued in 2010 which spelt out clearly the malpractices for profit-making MFIs: "where as these SHGs are being exploited by private Micro Finance Institutions (MFIs) through usurious interest rates and coercive means of recovery resulting in their impoverishment and in some cases leading to suicides ..." One is justified in asking "What was RBI doing in the meanwhile?" RBI's honeymoon with MFIs was reflected in its conspiracy of silence. But for the Andhra Governments ordinance which exposed the under-belly of profit-making MFIs, the exploitation of small borrowers by MFIs would have continued unabated. It is the subsequent MFI crisis which led to soul-searching. The Central Government woke up and has introduced in May 2012 a bill in Parliament which will empower RBI to regulate MFIs. The bill awaits legislative approval.

RBI was fully aware of the wrong doings of MFIs but maintained a profound silence. Dr Y.V. Reddy, former RBI Governor, later confessed that many financial experts believed, but did not have the courage to admit publicly, that microfinance is India's sub-prime. In fact MFIs are worse than moneylenders. Moneylender lends out of his own money, whereas here, MFIs are actually borrowing money from depositors and banks and lending the money. So, "MFIs is essentially a leveraged money lender". The studied silence of experts, including RBI, has cost, as the post-2010 crisis shows, the economy, particularly small borrowers a great deal. RBI seeks to take shelter under the fact that it had no power to regulate the MFIs. But the argument is specious. If RBI today regards MFI lending as sub-prime lending, surely it could have egged on the Government of India to take appropriate steps and take them immediately.

In fact, RBI's guilt runs much deeper. We are tempted to ask Dr Reddy: It is one thing to say that RBI had no statutory powers to regulate to MFIs; but was it obliged to support MFIs? This support came not only from RBI but also from public sector banks (PSBs), National Bank for Agriculture and Rural Development (NABARD) and Small Industries Development Bank of India (SIDBI). RBI could have stipulated that PSBs should lend only to non-profit MFIs. This systemic support perhaps also lent some respectability to non-profit MFIs. Public sector financial resources were thus merrily used to perpetuate usurious lending practices of MFIs, and to boost their private profits.

In the post-reform phase, RBI policy makers were soaked in market theology. Mindless implementation of Basel norms and blind belief in market-determined interest rates led to the emergence of inequitable interest rate structure. For instance, a small farmer was made to pay an interest rate of 12 per cent at a time when a high rated corporate entity could raise money from banks at 6 per cent. The truth finally dawned on RBI in 2007, when it admitted that this interest structure led to "cross subsidization of the economically well-off borrowers by the economically poor borrowers." Thus, it took two decades for RBI to correct the distortion in the interest rate structure.

RBI's honeymoon with the MFIs had not ended. The Malegam Committee has made some excellent recommendations regarding inspection and regulation of MFIs. But the main recommendation that MFIs could charge an interest rate of 24 per cent on individual loans is disturbing. This again reflects RBI's belief in "market determined" interest rates. RBI is quite sensitive to the corporate sector's demand for reduction of bank lending rates but not to small borrowers. Small borrowers from MFIs are not Schumpeterian heroes who can bear the burden of such high interest cost and yet make the enterprise viable. In other words, we are building non-viability into the enterprise for which small borrowers borrow from MFIs. It is high time that RBI revisited this recommendation of sanctifying the usurious lending rate of 24 per cent.

The recent revelations that the London Inter-bank Offered Rate or the Libor was rigged and manipulated should open the eyes of RBI. This rate was the axis around which the western financial markets revolved, and was venerated as an example of "market-determined" interest rate. The investigations of the scandal both in England and the U.S. have exploded the myth of market-determined rates. Barklays the first victim of the scandal had to pay a huge fine of $450 million.

These two factors—the exploding the myth of market-determined interest rates and the hard economic reality that rural enterprises cannot be viable at 24 per cent interest rate should prod RBI to rethink about the role of profit-making MFIs in rural finance. The rural sector has already its Shylocks in the form of moneylenders. There is no space for introducing a new breed of Shylocks blessed by Malegam Committee. Fortunately, India has a healthy home-grown segment of micro finance Public Sector Banks (PSBs), restructured Regional Rural Banks (RRBs), rejuvenated cooperative credit system, NABARD's Self-Help Groups (SHGs) Bank Linkages Programme (SBLP), which has emerged as a major channel of micro finance. Then there is the post office, which is already functioning as a semi-bank with its 1.55 lakh branches and some 16 crores customers. RBI could regain its lost credibility by focusing on the further development of this segment.

27

The Microfinance Mess

RECENT revelations of for-profit microfinance institutions (MFIs) have exposed naked exploitation by these institutions in the name of financial inclusion. Dr Y.V. Reddy, former Governor, Reserve Bank of India (RBI), recently said that these MFIs are worse than moneylenders. A moneylender lends out of his own money whereas here, MFIs were actually borrowing money from depositors and banks and then further lending the money. In retrospect, the Government of Andhra Pradesh deserves to be congratulated on its 2010 ordinance which spelt out clearly the malpractices of such MFIs. Whereas these self-help groups (SHGs) are being exploited by private MFIs through usurious interest rates and coercive means of recovery resulting in their impoverishment and in some cases leading to suicides the ordinance said. This triggered a crisis which almost paralysed for-profit MFIs, with banks reluctant to lend, repayments dwindling and depositors tending to withdraw their money. It is this shock therapy which led to subsequent soul-searching on the part of those MFIs, the promoters of which were fattening themselves off the sweat of poor borrowers. The Microfinance Institutions Network (MFIN), a grouping of for-profit micro lenders, has now set up a committee to look into these deficiencies. In fact the clout of these MFIs seems to be so strong that in spite of all that has been now exposed, some influential papers plead: Do not Kill Microfinance. The short answer to such pleas is: We do not want to kill these MFIs but we certainly want to prevent them from killing their poor borrowers.

No doubt the for-profit MFIs represent the predatory face of financial capitalism. But this was compounded by the institutional support which was extended to these MFIs. Such support came from the RBI, the public sector banks (PSBs), National Bank for Agriculture and Rural Development (NABARD) and Small Industries Development Bank of India (SIDBI). For instance, during 2008-09, banks extended loans of something like ₹ 3,700 crore. Why should PSBs extend loans to MFIs at something like 12 per cent, when they were fully aware that these funds would be on-lent by MFIs at 25 to 30 per cent? The answer is that such loans by PSBs to MFIs were treated as priority sector lending. So this had the blessings of RBI. Similarly, some equity or quasi-equity support came from SIDBI and NABARD, of course, at concessional rates. RBI could have stipulated that PSBs should lend only to not-for-profit category of MFIs. PSBs could have also stipulated, on their part, that the on-lending rate of beneficiary MFIs should not exceed say 17 or 18 per cent. This was not done. This systemic support perhaps also lent some respectability to for-profit MFIs. Thus public sector financial resources were used to perpetuate usurious lending practices of MFIs.

It is one thing to say that RBI had no statutory powers to regulate MFIs. But was it obliged to support for-profit MFIs? These questions must be answered by Dr Reddy, during whose tenure the MFI party began. RBI could have stipulated that PSBs should lend only to not-for-profit MFIs, fixing a ceiling on their on-lending rates. This support made the system, in a manner of speaking, a co-conspirator in this business of exploiting poor rural borrowers. Public funds were allowed to generate private profits. RBI has not covered itself in glory in this episode.

Because of obscenely high returns, stemming from exorbitant lending rates, for-profit MFIs have become attractive investment destinations for Private Equity and Venture Capitalists. The recent success of the initial public offering (IPO) of SKS Microfinance is a case in point. It attracted high profile investors like billionaire George Soros, venture capitalists Vinod Khosala and Infosys Founder Narayan Murthy. Alluding to this transformation of the humble animal microfinance, Muhammad Yunus, the father of microfinance movement said: "It is a complete detour and nothing but a quitting of microfinance mission."

Basically, lending to the rural poor at 30 or 40 per cent defies all economic logic. Our small rural borrowers are not Schumpeterian mini-heroes, who can make the project or activity for financing what they have borrowed, financially viable. In fact, by inflating interest cost, we are building *ab initio* non-viability into the project. Secondly, the engagement of for-profit MFIs with borrowers has been shallow based on touch and move on business models shorn of any development content. The average loans per client in both MFIs and SHGs have been low, between ₹ 3,500 and ₹ 5,000. The duration of the loan is short, typically one year or less. The small loan size and short duration do not enable most borrowers to do much except to ease liquidity problems. (*Microfinance India: State of the Sector Report*, 2008). It was M.L. Darling who wrote long ago that the Indian peasant is born in debt, lives in debt and dies in debt, thanks to the moneylender. Are we trying to promote the Darling syndrome?

Whatever RBIs Y.H. Malegam Committee has recommended, covers some ground towards reforming the for-profit MFIs. But it seems to have missed the central point. The public sector support to for-profit MFIs should be withdrawn forthwith. After all, why did PSBs begin to extend their support to such MFIs? Because these MFIs provided an easy escape route to their responsibility regarding meeting the priority sector credit target of 40 per cent. In doing so, we have landed ourselves into a greater mess. Then there was this façade of financial inclusion. This empirical experience has demonstrated that under such circumstances it is better not to have borrowed at all, at prohibitive costs, than borrowed and lost. It is better to remain excluded than included.

Where do we go from here? Indian policy makers must be reminded that India, unlike many other countries, say Bangladesh for example, has a healthy home grown segment of microfinance. PSBs, restructured regional rural banks (RRBs), rejuvenated cooperative credit system, NABARDs Self-Help Groups Bank Linkage Programme (SBLP) have emerged as a major channel of microfinance. Then there is the post office, which is already functioning as a semi-bank, with its 1.55 lakh branches and some 16 crore customers. This has great potential, given appropriate policy support, to emerge as a low-cost microfinance channel. The point is that these public or semi-public sector segments have successfully blended profitability criteria with social banking. Of course, not-for-profit MFIs are indeed welcome to join the stream. Our policy makers could do well to refocus their energies on further developing this segment, rather than trying to reform rouge MFIs. In the business of financial inclusion, there is enough space for not-for-profit MFIs but not for rogue MFIs.

III

Banking Policy

28

Think Global but Act Local

IN the first flush of enthusiasm of introducing banking sector reforms in the 1990s, our policy-makers were obsessed with implementing Basel norms and internalising international best practices. This mindless implementation of Basel norms and practices led to several distortions in policy which later proved to be harmful to the economy. Against this background, it is refreshing to find that Reserve Bank of India (RBI) is now making a plea for focusing on India-specific issues, notwithstanding global considerations. The *Report on Trend and Progress of Banking in India*, 2010-11 (TPBR), released in December 2011 puts it successfully: The surmise, therefore, is that Indian banks should increase their global presence. In the rapidly changing global financial landscape, it is imperative for the Indian banks to think global but act local! This change in the stance of banking policy was long overdue and welcome.

Among the more conspicuous distortions that resulted from the mindless adoption of Basel norms, two may be highlighted here: inequitable interest rate structure and disenfranchisement of small borrowers. The interest rate structure which emerged from the implementation of Basel norms was designed to pamper the private corporate sector, and which was biased against agricultural and small borrowers generally. For instance, a small farmer was made to pay an interest rate of 12 per cent at a time when a highly rated corporate entity could raise money from banks at 6 per cent. The RBI realised this later and admitted openly that in this interest rate structure there was cross subsidisation of economically well-off borrowers by the economically poor borrowers. RBI appointed a Working Group in April 2008 to look into this issue. As a result of the recommendations of this Working Group, banks switched over to the Base Rate System with effect from July 1, 2010. Thus it took two decades for the RBI to correct the distortion. Meanwhile, the small borrowers, particularly small farmers, were 'exploited' by the interest rate regime.

Perhaps the unkindest cut off the Basel bank culture induced by-product was the disenfranchisement of small farmers. 'Lean operations' required that banks should shed borrowal accounts. There was a dramatic decline in the number of small borrowal accounts with credit limits of ₹ 25,000; their number which had risen to 62.55 million in March 1992 dipped to only 36.87 million by March 2003. The credit outstanding of this category of accounts which formed nearly 22 per cent of total outstanding credit in 1992 plunged to only 5.2 per cent in 2003.

Public sector banks (PSBs) were trying to boost their profits by economies of exclusion. Contrast this with the obsessive concern of today's policy-makers—both the Government and RBI—with financial inclusion. It is against this background that the change in the banking policy stance, as articulated in the RBI's TPBR needs to be appreciated. First, about the strength of the Indian banking system. The banking system emerged largely unscathed from the global financial crisis of 2007-08. Despite the challenging headwinds from international developments, the performance of Indian banks remained robust in 2010-11.

The resilience of the banking system was marketed by improvement in the capital base, asset quality and profitability. Indian banks are adequately prepared for migration to Basel III regime. Quick assessments show that at the aggregate level Indian banks will not have any difficulty to adjusting to the new capital rules both in terms of quantum and quality. Thus Indian banks are comfortably placed in terms of compliance with the higher capital requirements. In regard to asset quality, both gross and net NPA (non-performing asset) ratios declined in 2010-11, from the previous year's level. Gross NPAs have been steadily declining from 15.7 per cent in 1997 to 2.25 per cent in 2011, but this does not reveal the underlying realities. Gross NPA ratio rose from 1.81 per cent in 2008 to 2.21 per cent in 2010. The Report exorts banks to step up their efforts to resolve the existing NPAs.

The profitability of banks improved both in terms of return on assets (RoA) and return on equity (RoE). Further, the banking system has registered an impressive improvement in productivity over the last 15 years and many of the productivity/efficiency indicators have moved closer to the global levels. The change in the banking policy stance is clearly reflected in the following statements: "The banking sector is a key driver of inclusive growth". The most significant task of the Indian banking sector is to ensure "that banking products and services are made available to every individual in the country efficiently to achieve total financial inclusion. In the next decade the major challenge before banks is financing of the millions in the unorganised sector, self-employed in the micro and small business sector, the small and marginal farmers as also rural share-croppers in the agricultural sector. Other challenges include financing affordable housing and education needs of low income households.

It is good that RBI has spelt out in clear terms the future agenda for PSBs. Even now there are some PSBs who grumble that 'no-frills accounts' are acting as a drag on their profits and that the Government should subsidise them. Such bankers should now get ready to obey the mandate of RBI. In the medium term, expected positive economic performance, strong savings growth spurred by the favourable demographic dividend, emphasis on expansion of physical infrastructure and the extent of financial exclusion to be bridged—all these factors will pave the way for healthy growth of the banking system.

In the Basel bank culture inspired euphoria some Indian policy-makers had delusions of grandeur. Indian banks should grow to a size 'too big to fail'. The global financial crisis of 2008 exploded this myth about the size. RBI now takes a balanced view it is unlikely that any of the Indian banks will come in the top ten of the global league even after reasonable consolidation. Indian banks should look inwards rather than outwards, focusing their efforts on deeper financial penetration.

The latest *Financial Stability Report* (issue no. 4) released by the RBI in December 2011 endorses this assessment of the strength of the Indian banking system. "Indian banks remain robust, notwithstanding a decline in CRAR and spurt in a NPA levels in the recent past. Increased capital needs and liquidity requirements under Basel III will need to be carefully phased in." The tragedy of banking sector reforms in the post-1990s phase has been that policy-makers tried to mimic western banking, particularly, American banking models. This led to the kind of distortions discussed above. A redeeming feature of the reform scenario is RBI's introspection and transparency. It has admitted openly the mistakes committed and set out to correct distortions. The interest rate structure is a case in point. RBI's call for total financial inclusion articulated forcefully in this Report, one hopes, will spur all PSBs to achieve the goal.

29

The Issues Facing Heads of Banks

WHAT are the current issues facing heads of banks? The Indian Institute of Banking and Finance has put together responses of 14 banks 13 public sector banks (PSBs) and one private sector bank to the Institute's questionnaire on the subject. The issues discussed include regulatory capital risk measurement, base rate system, customer service banking utility and agricultural finance, role of rating agencies. Dr R. Bhaskaran, CEO of the Institute deserves to be commended on collecting the views of heads of banks and putting them in the public domain by publishing them in the Institute's journal *Bank Quest* (January-March 2011 issue). It is important to highlight the issues that bankers have spoken about and the issues that they have chosen not to speak about. This response reflects the priority that heads of banks attach to various issues.

In fact the bankers responses need to be analysed in conjunction with the Reserve Bank of India's (RBI) *Financial Stability Report* released in June 2011, which we discussed earlier in this column (*Financial Stability and Economic Growth*, July 5, 2011). This Report reflects the policy makers' priorities. In the ultimate analysis, RBI's policies are to be implemented by banks and hence banks' priorities and commitment are crucial. We would seek to show that priorities of banks seem to differ from priorities of RBI.

One general comment on bankers' perception of the future growth of the banking industry is that bankers seemed to be Basel obsessed. India-specific issues seem to have taken a back-seat, in the minds of bankers. This is a hangover the financial sector reforms introduced since 1991. The concept of regulatory capital on a standardised basis, i.e., Basel-I was implemented in 1992. The implementation of Basel-II which defined capital charge in more sophisticated terms started in 2005. In response to the global financial crisis of 2008,

Bank for International Settlements (BIS) has now proposed Basel-III measures that call for higher regulatory capital in due course of time; implementation of this proposal, in phases, will start from January 2013. The heads of banks seem to be comfortable with these higher capital requirements, although it would limit business expansion of banks. While private banks are able to access equity market for augmenting capital PSB are hopeful of capital infusion by Government of India.

Again, take risk management. Measurement of risk is an important aspect of risk management. Heads of banks agree that the goal of advanced measurement approach needs to be reached, despite there being many challenges. In this context, it is necessary to remind bankers, that blind adoption of Basel norms or measurement tools may lead to distortions, as it did in the case of interest rates. While a triple A rated corporate entity could raise money from banks at 6 per cent, the small farmer was made to pay 12 per cent. This resulted in the emergence of inequitable interest rate structure in which small borrowers subsidised large borrowers. The RBI was honest enough to admit the distortion and replaced Benchmark Prime Lending Rates System (BPLRs) with the Base Rate system. But it took two decades to correct the distortion.

The adoption of Basel (norms) techniques should be tempered by Indian realities.

RBI's stability Report has highlighted the major concerns of commercial banks: increased reliance on market borrowings to fund assets, increasing imbalances in the maturity profile of assets and liabilities, and potential additions to asset impairment. Strangely enough bankers responses do not discuss any of these issues.

The most conspicuous omission by the bankers is the subject of financial inclusion and associated issues. Both Government of India and RBI are pursuing this objective with a missionary zeal and therefore one thought it would be on top of the agenda of bankers. This is not so. PSBs are expected to cover some 73,000 additional villagers by March 2012. Some 75 million no-frills bank accounts have been opened but about 85 per cent of these accounts are not operational and the average deposit is only ₹ 11 because the account holders are not involved in any economic activities. What purpose on earth such 'dead' or 'near-dead' accounts serve? Recently RBI has pulled up banks for paying lip service to financial inclusion and asked them to activate these accounts. Some critics also argue that PSBs are frittering away their energies on fringe activities at the cost of core activities. For instance, State Bank of India (SBI) has completed 5 million Aadhar unique identity cards enrollments, making it the largest non-government registrar in the country. Can we deduce from these attitudes of bankers that their commitment to financial inclusion is less than total? One wonders.

Of course, bankers have discussed agricultural finance. They have asserted the agricultural lending is a viable business proposition. This is rather strange because since nationalisation of 14 major commercial banks in 1969, our banking policy has focused its attention on financing agriculture or priority sectors more generally. Does it require four decades to discover that agriculture lending is a viable proposition? This attitude again is a hangover of the Basel syndrome, that agriculture is a more risky business. The very concept of 'risk' as embodied in the Basel theology should be made to stand on its head. I have discussed this whole theme in the monograph on 'Risk Philosophy' prepared for the National Bank for Agriculture and Rural Development (NABARD). However, it is encouraging to note that bankers are making efforts to reach the small and marginal farmers, through product innovation, special branches, special drives, etc.

Let there be no misunderstanding. Basel norms have to be necessarily observed but this should not be at the cost of India-specific core issues. Financial inclusion becomes meaningful only if the millions of no-frills accounts are activated, thereby triggering some economic activities.

30

The Bank Customer is King?

ARE we really pampering the customer of banks, particularly public sector banks (PSBs)? This is the question we are likely to raise when we see yet another 'Report of the Committee on Customer Service in Banks' submitted by M. Damodaran, former Chairman of the Securities and Exchange Board of India (SEBI) last month. There was the Talwar Committee on customer service in banks appointed in 1975, the Goiporia Committee appointed in 1990; the Tarapore Committee appointed in 2004, made recommendations which led to the formation of board level committees for monitoring customer service in banks. Are we treating the bank customer as king? Not in reality, alas!

The Damodaran Committee appointed by the Reserve Bank of India (RBI) in May 2010, aroused particular interest because the first among its six terms of reference was the following:

> To review the existing system of attending to customer service in banks approach, attitude and fair treatment to customers from retail, small and pensioners segment.

After perusing through this scholarly Report of some 150 pages one is disappointed that this specific issue has not been adequately addressed.

Let there be no misunderstanding. It is a scholarly Report and the Committee has done its homework. It has sought guidance from 'international best practices'. The United Nations Guidelines for consumer protection, the Financial Services Authority, UK's (FSA) fairness commitment to be made by banks, the Community Reinvestment Act (CRA) of USA which prohibits discrimination by banks against low and moderate income neighbourhoods, all these were analysed by the Committee to derive policy inputs. The

Committee has made excellent recommendations for streamlining Grievance Redressal System in banks, Banking Ombudsman Scheme, Banking Technology and Role of Boards of Banks in customer service.

The Committee deserves to be congratulated on the high quality of the Report.

This article seeks to highlight the fact that the Committee has failed to address adequately the problems faced by the small borrower the *aam aadmi* precisely what the terms of reference mentioned above required.

Glancing through the recommendations, one gets the impression that most bank customers are familiar with mobile banking, and receiving and sending short message service (SMS): if a bank wants to make an account inoperative, banks must intimate the customer by SMS; not maintaining the minimum balance should be intimated by SMS; small discounts should be offered to customers to promote electronic payments; provision to apply for small retail loan should be available in bank's portal and Internet banking; and so on.

No doubt your vegetable vendor may be using mobile phone today: but is he capable of sending and receiving SMSes? The perception of banking business by RBI today is reflected in the following statement of a Senior Officer: "Assets with banks are maintained more in digitised rather than physical form, transactions are carried out over technology-enabled platforms/applications and communications are over electronic modes...There are newer products and channels of delivery. Networked environment has enabled delivery of banking services at the door step of the customer. Anywhere and anytime banking with core banking and newer delivery channels viz., ATM online banking and mobile banking etc. have provided convenience of banking to the customer and an increasing number of people rely upon the convenience and ease of internet banking services, in their business as well as daily life". (Secured Online Banking and Customer Convenience G. Padmanabhan, *RBI Bulletin,* August 2011). It is such a perception of high profile banking which colours most of the recommendations of the Damodaran Committee. Are we focusing on elite banking or high profile banking, at the cost of core banking?

One begins to wonder. Let us discuss the following three core banking issues.

First KYC (Know your Customer) Norms. Dr S.S. Tarapore the veteran Central Banker, has been carrying on a one-man campaign to expose how many PSBs are using this instrument to shoo away the small customer from accessing banking services. He has put into public domain several concrete cases to demonstrate that small customers are prevented from opening accounts on flimsy grounds: authenticating residential address or even spelling mistakes in their names or localities in which they reside. The victims include domestic help, drivers or labourers working with a construction firm. In this sense, Dr Tarapore has bitterly argued that KYC has become a synonym for 'Kill your Customer'. One does appreciate the security concerns but the managers at the branch level should be discerning enough to discriminate between *bona fide* cases and suspicious cases. The Damodaran Committee does refer to reforming 'attitudinal aspects' and 'rude Relationship Managers' but does not offer any concrete recommendations to redress them. It does, however, recommends that "self-attested photograph and address proof should be treated as sufficient KYC to open no frills account". In cities like Mumbai where 40 per cent of the population lives in slums or semi-slums, it may be difficult to produce documents re: residence. The point is bank managers should be flexible in appraising such documents. Financial inclusion campaigns will be meaningful only if managers adopt a helpful attitude towards opening accounts.

Secondly, on the positive side, take financial inclusion. Under this campaign, some 75 million no-frills bank accounts have been opened. Unfortunately, about 85 per cent of these accounts are not operational and the average deposit per account is ₹ 11 because the account holders are not involved in any economic activities. What purpose on earth such 'dead' or 'near dead' accounts serve? Recently RBI has pulled up banks for paying lip service to financial inclusion and asked them to activate these accounts. Is this issue not part of customer service?

Thirdly, in the not-too-distant past—some public sector banks played a critical role in agricultural development. They appointed their own agricultural officers and provided extension services. This extension-linked credit was a great success. Today, with the Government de-emphasising the role of the extension worker, there is a gap which could be usefully filled by banks. Agricultural growth is necessary not only for food security but also for overall growth of the economy.

The main point to drive home is that when we talk of customer services of banks in India, we should grow out of the 'international banking practices' syndrome. India-specific issues should receive equal emphasis. Serving high networth individuals (HNIs) or high profile bank customer is indeed banks' legitimate business. But this should not overshadow the core and traditional banking business, including serving and nourishing the small borrowers. Out banking culture should be so shaped that it blends the dual functions.

31

Financial Inclusion or Tokenism?

OUR Eleventh Five Year Plan (2007-2012) aims at bringing about inclusive growth in the real sector. In the context of the policy paradigm of inclusive growth in the real sector, financial inclusion has become a policy priority. The basic idea is simple: access to affordable finance may enable the poor, especially the rural poor, to undertake economic activities like self-employment, or micro businesses. The broader perspective of financial inclusion is provided by the Rangarajan Commission: "financial inclusion is considered a prerequisite for empowerment, employment, economic growth, poverty reduction, and social cohesion." A rather tall order indeed!

Financial inclusion is thus the process of ensuring access to credit, or financial services generally, needed by vulnerable groups such as weaker sections and low income groups at affordable cost, from the mainstream institutions, like commercial banks, regional rural banks (RRBs), and cooperatives. Reserve Bank of India (RBI) has taken a number of measures to accelerate this process of financial inclusion by setting specific targets of coverage of population by public sector banks (PSBs). A major change introduced by RBI is that such coverage could take place not necessarily through a brick and mortar branch but also through any of the various forms of information and communication technology (ICT) based models like business correspondents (BCs). Under this BC model banks have been permitted to use the services of various entities like the individual *kirana* medical/fair price shop owners, agents of small saving schemes, functionaries of well-run Self-Help Groups (SHGs) linked to banks.

Two funds were set up with NABARD: first, Financial Inclusion Fund for meeting the cost of developmental and promotional interventions for facilitating financial inclusion, and secondly, Financial Inclusion Technology Fund to meet the cost of technology adoption. The overall Corpus of these funds was ₹ 500 crore each: these were enhanced by ₹ 100 crore each in 2010-11.

In November 2009, the RBI advised banks to draw up a road map to provide, by March 2011, banking services in every village with a population of over 2,000. The target date has now been postponed to March 2012. About 73,000 villages have been allocated to various banks for provision of banking services.

While, in principle, the concept of financial inclusion is indeed incontrovertible, it is necessary to introspect on whether the way we are going about to achieve the results is the right way. Does the target-based approach, targets in terms of villages to be covered, or number of accounts to be opened, dilute the substance of inclusion? In this zeal for 100 per cent coverage, is the movement being reduced to tokenism? This article seeks to address these issues.

In retrospect, it can be seen that much before financial inclusion became internationally fashionable, the authors of nationalisations of banks in 1969, emerge as pioneers of financial inclusion. The expansion of branches of public sector banks was phenomenal in the post-nationalisation period, unprecedented in the history of world banking. Banking growth in this era was in a manner of speaking organic. Banks were allocated areas for expansion like Lead Districts. Further expansion was left to banks concerned: each bank would decide on whom to lend; how much to lend and so on. In other words, normal banking practices governed the expansion of banking.

In contract, the emphasis now seems to be on quantities. How many accounts has a bank opened? Since the inception of the scheme in November 2005, 50.6 million no-frills accounts, which banks are required to open with very low or even nil balances have been opened by banks, upto March 2010, with an outstanding balance of ₹ 5,386 crore. Further more, in 2009-10, banks were advised to provide small over drafts in such accounts, by March 2010 banks had provided 0.18 million over drafts with a total amount of ₹ 28 crore. General purpose credit cards (GCC) offered by banks at their rural and semi-urban branches are in the nature of revolving credit, entitling the holder to withdraw upto the limit sanctioned (₹ 25,000). By March 2010, banks had provided credit aggregating ₹ 635 crore for 3.5 million GCC accounts. This is a result of 'command performance', a case of directed credit. This massive target of number of accounts to be opened is putting a strain of banks' resources, both human and financial. The Ministry of Finance is planning to compensate PSBs for this additional burden imposed on them in terms of rural penetration.

Our submission is that RBI's approach to financial inclusion in the sense of universal or near universal coverage of households is flawed, or basically misconceived. Banking sector resources are, and would continue to be, limited. Optimum utilisation of banking sector resources would demand a selective approach to credit extension. Ideally credit should chase productive activities and if this is ensured, we could promote optimal use of banking sector resources. Spreading banking sector resources too thinly, which universal coverage necessarily implies, would not lead to optimise growth.

However, today financial inclusion has been reduced to a game of numbers, a mere tokenism. Take, for instance, 'no-frills accounts', we have discussed above. As Dr Tarapore, former Deputy Governor, has pointed out, only a tenth of these accounts are operational. What purpose on earth 90 per cent of such 'near dead' accounts serve? Only RBI could provide an answer to this question. Because these accounts have stemmed from 'targets' and not grown organically, they are in a sorry state.

The point is let us not pursue the shadow of universal coverage but seize the substance of banking. Let RBI allocate areas to different banks for penetration but, leave the selection of borrowers to banks. Let there by no insistence on numbers. Then there will be the normal banking practices which govern the selection of borrowers, the quantum of credit to be given and so on. This approach would bring about healthy banking growth, facilitating growth in the real sector.

32

Bad Loans and Banking Culture

BAD debts or non-performing assets (NPAs), as they are called in banking jargon, of public sector banks (PSBs) are in the news again. NPAs have been increasing over the year, agriculture and small-scale industries (SSIs) sectors accounting for about half the total. The instinctive reaction of the so-called banking intellectuals and media is that Government's push for financial inclusion and priority sector lending is driving PSBs to face such increase in NPAs. Should we therefore slow down our efforts towards financial inclusion?

This article seeks to argue that bad debts are not the exclusive 'virtue' of agriculture or SSIs sectors. Large and medium industries are as much vulnerable to bad debts as are agriculture and SSIs. So let us not throw out the baby along with the bath water. Secondly, the overall level of NPAs is even now within the 'comfort' level. There is no need to be panicky. Third, what may be broadly called banking culture—the mode and manner of conducting banking business is as much important as other factors in determining the level of bad debts. Hence we must pay adequate attention to improve our banking culture to manage our level of bad debts.

Proper Perspective

The Reserve Bank of India (RBI) puts the bad debts position in a proper perspective. The gross NPAs of public sector banks rose from ₹ 40,452 crore in 2008 to ₹ 45,156 crore in 2009. On the other hand, NPAs as a proportion of gross advances declined from 2.2 per cent to 2 per cent. RBI stresses another additional point. Indian banks—all banks including PSBs—recovered a higher amount of NPAs during 2008-09 than that during the previous year: thus the trend of improvement in the asset quality of banks continued. Admittedly, in terms of gross NPAs of all scheduled commercial banks (SCBs), there was an increase. RBI provides an explanation: "In this context, it may be noted that in the present context of financial turmoil, some slippage in NPAs could be expected. Nevertheless, it may be noted that this slippage was moderate as compared to the problems faced by banks all over the world" (*Report on Trend and Progress of Banking in India 2008-09*, p.128).

International Best Practices Syndrome

In introducing financial sector reforms since 1991, our financial policy-makers have come to rely on international best practices. For instance, we find more offen RBI issuing guidelines to banks based on documents of Bank for International Settlements (BIS). This syndrome has cost us dearly, as we will demonstrate presently.

The global financial crisis of 2008 has exposed the weaknesses of American banking practices. The Financial Crisis Inquiry Commission, appointed in January 2011 has cited several of the banking malpractices of banks. More recently, the Levin-Coburn Report has given graphic expression to these malpractices. Blame for this mess (2088 financial crisis) lies everywhere—from federal regulators who cast a blind eye to Wall Street bankers who let greed run wild. It shows without a doubt the lack of ethics in some of our financial institutions who embraced known conflicts of interest to accomplish wealth for themselves not caring about the outcome for their customers. Is this the kind of culture that we are trying to imitate?

Banking Culture: New and Old

It is fascinating to compare the banking culture of especially the PSBs in the pre-reform period and the reform-tainted culture in the post-1991 period.

Take the case of interest rates. Why was the farmer required to pay an interest rate of 12 per cent, at a time when high rated corporate could raise money from banks at 6 per cent? The concept of risk adapted from the Basel model was faulty. It took two decades for RBI to correct this distortion in the interest rate structure. It was only in 2010 that the 'base' rate replaced the faulty Benchmark Prime Lending Rate (BPLR).

Second, RBI's statute that mandates the responsibility of promoting rural credit on the Central Bank. The All-India Rural Credit Survey of 1956 stipulated: "Cooperation has failed: but co-operation must succeed". Since then RBI has acted as a guardian-angel of the farmer ensuring concessional lending rates to rural borrowers. But today, a high-powered RBI committee—the Malegam Committee—has the audaucity to recommend that microfinance institutions (MFIs) can charge an interest rate of absurdly high level of 26 per cent. Even triple 'A rated corporates would rebel against such usurious lending rates. What a change of banking culture at RBI!

Third, the Punjab National Bank (PNB) has always been aggressive in lending to agriculture, much before priority sector targets become mandatory. Interestingly enough, the recovery rate in respect of agricultural lending was as high as 95 per cent. Those who complain that agricultural sector is a drag on recovery should educate themselves by the empirical experience of PNB. They did not have the notorious 'recovery agents' of the type that some foreign banks employ for recovery of car loans etc. and some bigger micro-credit institutions (MFIs) had in Andhra Pradesh.

Fourth, today we bemoan the act that Chief of State Bank of India (SBI) is paid much less than the CEOs of foreign banks or even of ICICI or HDFC. The underlying assumption seems to be that the commitment to the job varies in direct proportion to the size of emoluments. This logic is flawed. Take for instance, the pioneers of public sector banking. The phenomenal expansion of banking in the post-nationalisation period is unprecedented in the history of world banking. The very concept of taking banking to the people, the techniques employed to extend the reach of banks, the training imparted to personnel involved in this gigantic task and the trials and tribulations of the whole exercise are documented in the book: 'Taking Banking to the People' brought out by the National Institute of Bank Managements (NIBM), Pune, in 2002. Banking officials, at that period of time, were not being paid princely sums. The total commitment of all those involved and the dedication with which they pursued the objective is indeed admirable. What we need today is the 'small borrower-friendly' banking culture.

Finally, much before the Grameen Bank of Bangladesh became famous, the Syndicate Bank had started banking for the poor: its pigmy deposits, its opening of small counters in the vegetable market to lend to vendors in the morning and to receive repayments in the evening, penetrating small, inaccessible villages—all these are documented by Dr Thingalaya, former Chairman of the Syndicate Bank. This should be compulsory reading for all young professionals recruited to work in PSBs.

Overall, the point to drive home is that 'such small borrower-friendly banking culture' would go a long way towards reducing bad loans.

33

Priority Sectors and Banking Policy

THE Reserve Bank of India (RBI) had issued in July 2012 revised guidelines to banks specifying what constitutes priority sectors. The main change that these guidelines seek to bring about is that loans to large corporates like dairying or fertiliser distributing companies will no longer qualify for being classified as direct lending to agriculture. The basic idea is to goad public sector banks (PSBs) to lend to farmers directly in greater measure to meet the priority sector credit target of 40 per cent of total credit. The priority sectors include agriculture and allied activities like animal husbandry, small enterprises, and retail trade. It is estimated that if the revised guidelines are implemented, the magnitude of flow of credit to these sectors will increase by around ₹ 50,000 crore.

The RBI proposal should be viewed as part of the 'learning process' of RBI and as part of the macro banking policy. Public memory may be short 'but not the researchers'. In the first flush of enthusiasm of implementing banking reforms in the early 1990s, RBI policy-makers were intoxicated with market theology and were keen on mimicking British or American banking models. Directed credit symbolised by the priority sector credit target of 40 per cent was a 'dirty phrase'. At the same time the policy-makers were not bold enough to openly do away with such credit targets. They adopted a more subtle way of de-emphasising priority sectors. Many PSBs defaulted on the 40 per cent target and RBI winked at the default. Not only that, in a bid to boost their profits, following British or American models, PSBs got rid of a large number of small borrowal accounts. In effect, small borrowers including small farmers were disenfranchised. All this has been well documented. A more concrete evidence of RBI's policy of financial 'exclusion' during this phase was that RBI ceased to discuss credit allocation to priority sectors. Traditionally, RBI's *Annual Reports* devoted a couple of pages to discuss the share of priority sectors in total credit, and how many PSBs have defaulted on the target and so on. RBI was now content to devote one line to this subject in its *Annual Report*: "The data regarding sectoral distribution of credit are given in Table."

RBI's other subtle method of de-emphasising credit was to dilute the rigour of the target by widening the definition of what constitutes priority sectors. That is when corporates connected directly or indirectly with agriculture were included: dairying or fertiliser distributing companies. What RBI's July 2012 guidelines are aimed at is to correct this distortion. In this sense, this process is RBI's learning experience. The worst was yet to come. Profit-making Micro Finance institutions (MFIs) were brought into the net. Credit extended by PSBs to MFIs was included in the priority sector credit. PSBs thus found it convenient to meet the 40 per cent credit target by lending large amounts to these MFIs. For instance, in 2008-09, an amount of ₹ 3,732 crore was extended by banks as loans to MFIs. Public sector resources were thus merrily used, in the garb of priority sector lending, to perpetuate usurious lending practices of MFIs and to boost the latter's private profits. How PSBs involved in this exercise suffered in the aftermath of the 2010 MFI crisis is now part of India's financial history.

Alas! All this changed when the 11th Five Year Plan (2007-08 to 2011-12) emphasised inclusive growth in the real sector. Financial inclusion as a consequence became imperative and RBI policy-makers had to beat a hasty retreat.

While on this subject we must pay a tribute to the vision of policy-makers of the 1970s. Much before financial inclusion became fashionable internationally, these policy-makers had taken concrete steps to usher in financial inclusion: nationalisation of major banks in 1969, phenomenal bank branch expansion programme unprecedented in the history of world banking and fixing credit targets with a view to ensure wider disbursal of bank credit. These concerted efforts resulted in bringing about a structural transformation in the deployment of bank credit. For instance, the share of large and medium industries in total commercial bank credit which was around 61 per cent in

March 1968 declined significantly to 38 per cent in June 1982. Simultaneously, the share of priority sectors rose from 11 per cent to 36 per cent during this period. No private sector banks, including foreign banks, could have achieved this remarkable feat.

The Raghuram Rajan Committee shows its blissful innocence of India's banking history when it states: "The majority of this committee does not see a compelling reason for continuing government ownership of financial institutions. The point is that India has evolved its own brand of commercial banking linked to development and those experts brought up on the diet of British or American model of banking cannot appreciate the subtleties of India's banking system. Economic history provides enough evidence to show that private banks and/or foreign banks, by their very nature of objectives cannot promote development. Foreign banks were operating for many years in many of the former British colonies in Africa but these were catering primarily to large corporate of the expatriate businesses and hence the 'native' economy continued to remain on the fringe of modern banking.

The central point is that our future banking reforms should be built on the 'small borrower-friendly banking culture' which is now embedded in the system. In principle, the concept of financial inclusion is incontrovertible. But it is necessary to introspect on whether we are going about to achieve the results the right way. RBI's approach to financial inclusion in the sense of universal or near universal coverage, we submit, is flawed. Banking sector resources are limited and hence optimum utilisation of banking sector resources would demand a selective approach to credit extension.

Ideally, credit should chase productive activities. In this sense bringing priority sectors into the fold of modern banking is the first step. But this is not enough. Banks should also seek to extend technical help to small borrowers to upgrade the activities they are financing. This applies not only to agriculture but also to other activities: micro enterprises, self-employed persons. The *gram sevak* or village level worker was a crucial link in the Green Revolution phase between the borrower and the agencies concerned with farm technology. He now belongs to an extinct species. Our banking policy should aim at filling this vacuum of technological advice, not only for farm but also to non-farm activities.

34

Banking Reforms

Foreign versus Desi Consultants

THE recent directive by the Finance Ministry to public sector banks (PSBs) to implement the Report prepared by the Boston Consulting Group (BCG) on improving banking operations has raised the basic question of who should be preferred; foreign or *desi* experts? The Report exhorts banks "to strive for excellence on five dimensions": branch sales and service, new channels, lean operations, organisation design and bad debt-management". The Report also calls for a need to change the compensation structure, "Long overdue, the public sector urgently needs an adjustment in its compensation structure. The government should introduce performance-linked compensation framework for PSBs...."

An enterprising journalist has dug out a directive issued by former finance secretary Arun Ramanathan in 2007-08 asking banks to steer clear of foreign consultants. He had written to all bank chiefs to stress that we have plenty of internal or *desi* talent and therefore do not require advice from external agency on how to run a bank.

Advice from foreign agencies, with no roots in the economy has often led to harmful results, rather than helping the economy. This can be illustrated with two concrete cases. First, mindless implementation of Basel norms in the banking sector in the early 1990s led to the emergence of an inequitable interest rate structure, a structure designed to pamper the private corporate sector, and which was biased against agricultural and small borrowers generally. For instance, a small farmer was made to pay an interest rate of 12 per cent at time when a highly rated corporate entity could raise money from banks at 6 per cent. As eventually admitted by Reserve Bank of India (RBI) this led to cross subsidisation of the economically well-off borrowers by poor borrowers. It took RBI two decades to realise the mistake and to correct it by establishing a Base Rate System in 2010. The 'exploitation' of the small borrower in the medium term is thus obvious.

The 'Basel bank culture', if one might use the term, produced several distortions which proved to be destructive. Take for instance, credit to priority sectors. Directed credit is bad and commercial banks started willfully defaulting in the early 1990s on the credit target of 40 per cent to priority sectors. RBI winked at the default. Not only that RBI stopped discussing the subject of sectoral deployment of bank credit in its *Annual Reports*!

The worst was yet to come 'lean operations' required that banks should shed small borrowal accounts. The unkindest cut of the Basel bank culture induced by-products was the disenfranchisement of small farmers. There was a dramatic decline in the number of small borrowal accounts with credit limits of ₹ 25,000: their number which had reached 62.55 million in March 1992 dipped to only 36.87 million by March 2003. The credit outstanding of this category of accounts which formed nearly 22 per cent of total outstanding credit in 1992 dipped to only 5.2 per cent in 2003. PSBs were trying to boost their profits by economies of 'exclusion'. Contrast this with today's stance of policy makers, both Government of India and RBI, who are crying hoarse for financial inclusion. The policy-makers in the 1990s displayed a weakness for 'foreign advice' and the economy paid a heavy price for this weakness.

In retrospect, the most amusing episode is the World Bank's (WB) advice on Indian banking sector reforms. In 2002, the WB had organised a conference on India's financial sector. The conference papers were published in 2005 with the title: India's Financial Sector, Recent Reforms, Future Challenges. Today, the WB's assessment of India's financial sector appears amateurish, doctrinaire, and bereft of any insights into the realities. Obsession to pamper the private corporate sector and a congenital dislike of public sector are writ large on these papers. The WB argued that the private corporate sector "has not received the credit at the expected level". This was contrary to facts. Finally, the WB stated: "Equally, there is a need to deal with the country's public sector banks and financial institutions: there are good reasons to doubt whether government control can be made consistent with efficiency and commercialisation of these institutions." The final blow was the following statement: "Banking system distress in India is considerable both in absolute terms and when compared with distress faced by many of the East Asian countries on the eve of their crisis. Much of India's banking system is affected by a weak credit culture, poor risk assessment and management, supervision and regulation that is not fully in line with international standards and an inefficient legal and judicial framework". Is private management and control the paragon of efficiency? The WB experts could not even dream that the global financial crisis would prove them wrong!

In 2008 when icons of American and European financial institutions—commercial banks, investment banks, mortgage houses and insurance companies—collapsed like a pack of cards, the Indian financial system stood unscathed. Professor Joseph Stiglitz, the Nobel Laureate, in an interview to an Indian TV channel said: "The U.S. financial system collapsed because we did not have a Dr. Reddy at the helm." The reference was to Dr Y.V. Reddy former Governor of RBI, and there cannot be a better tribute to the management of the Indian financial system.

Finally, a word about the salary structure. In the process of implementing banking sector reforms, we have unfortunately tried to mimic many American banking practices. Some Indian reformers quote with glee American management Guru James Goldsmith's well-known statement. "If you pay peanuts, you only get monkeys." It is time we debunk this myth.

Competence, efficiency and a sense of commitment to the job do not vary with the size of the salary packet. It is pointless to compare salaries of say, the CEO of State Bank of India (SBI), or even the Governor of RBI with those of CEOs of Bank of America or Standard Chartered. India's banking history is a glorious example of total commitment and dedication of professionals. The phenomenal expansion of banking in India in the post-nationalisation period, both in terms of widening and deepening the banking system is unprecedented in the history of world banking. Bringing the rural sector into the mainstream banking was a stupendous achievement. The travails and tribulations of banking officials involved in this dramatic transformation are chronicled in the book: 'Taking Banking to the People' published by National Institute of Bank Management. It hardly needs to be added that officials at that point of time were not being paid princely sums.

The plea for eschewing obscenely high salaries should not be construed to mean that there is no case for appropriately raising the size of emoluments in the public sector. The central point is that reforms should be designed in the broader context of the moral ethos and value system of the society; and in this sense *desi* experts are better placed to offer appropriate advice.

35

Performance of Banking Sector: 2011-12

THE global banking system witnessed several setbacks in 2011 and 2012 as it was affected by tepid recovery in global growth, reemergence of the euro area sovereign debt crisis and deleveraging risks for global banks. This resulted in keeping the international financial markets and the banking system volatile during the period. Fortunately, the Indian banking industry remained largely insulated from the global financial turbulence. The Indian banking sector which successfully withstood the global financial crisis in 2008-09 has now started showing some signs of stress. This is clearly brought out by the analysis of the Reserve Bank of India (RBI): *Report on Trend and Progress of Banking in India: 2011-12*, released in November 2012.

Performance of Indian banks was on the whole good but there are problems to be tackled. Operational domestic environment was challenging with high inflation and decelerating GDP growth. During 2011-12 the two major indicators of profitability namely, return on assets (RoA) and return of equity (RoE) dipped marginally. Public sector banks RoA dipped from 0.96 per cent in 2010-11 to 0.88 per cent and RoE from 16.90 to 15.33 per cent. An encouraging development was that operating efficiency of banks in terms of cost-to-income ratio witnessed an improvement. Indian banks remained well-capitalised; all scheduled commercial banks have become Basel II compliant. In May 2012 the RBI came out with final guidelines for implementation of Basel III. These will become effective from January 2013. Concerns about growing non-performing assets (NPAs) loomed large. Gross NPAs as per cent of gross advances increased from 2.4 per cent in 2010-11 to 3.3 per cent in 2011-12. Banks exposure to the stressed state electricity boards and airline companies added to the deterioration in the asset quality of banks.

In recent years restructuring of advances has been one of the important channels used by banks to contain the deterioration in asset quality caused by the increase in NPAs. The steep increase in gross NPAs in 2011-12 was accompanied by a considerable pick up in the growth of restructured advances. During 2011-12 the total amount of NPAs recovered through Securitization and Reconstruction of Financial Assets and Enforcement of Security Interest (SARFAESI) Act, Debt Recovery Tribunals (DRTs) and Lok Adalats registered a decline compared with the previous years. Of the total amount recovered through these channels, recoveries under the SARFAESI Act constituted 70 per cent.

During 2011-12 total priority sector NPAs increased at a significantly higher rate than the growth of credit to the priority sector. However, the share of priority sector in total NPAs declined compared with the previous year.

Ironically, public and private sector banks' advances to priority sectors were lower than the credit target of 40 per cent of adjusted net bank credit; for public sector bank the share was 37.2 per cent.

The other areas on which the Report focuses is financial inclusion: though significant progress has been made in expanding the coverage of banking we have yet to achieve 'meaningful financial inclusion'. All public and private sector banks were asked to put in place Board approved three year Financial Inclusion Plans (FIPs) beginning from April 2010. The progress during the last two years has been quite impressive. Penetration of banking has increased many-fold in rural areas. At the end of March 2012, villages covered through business correspondents (BCs) constituted more than 80 per cent of the total member of villages covered under the FIPs. At the end of March 2012, the total number of no-frills accounts had surpassed 130 million, with the total amount in these accounts adding up to ₹ 1.20 billion. However, the catch is that only 2 per cent of these no-frills accounts had overdraft facility. Banks should therefore now address the issue of making these accounts active, if financial inclusion has to become meaningful. In the coming years banks have to focus on multiplying the number and value of transactions in the no-frills accounts.

Another innovative institutional instrument devised to facilitate bank penetration merits mention here. The Self-Help Group (SHG)-bank linkage programme started in 1992 by NABARD involves three agencies: the SHGs, commercial banks and non-government organisations (NGOs). Although the progress of this linkage programme was rather slow initially, it gained momentum after 1999. Today, at the end of March 2012 about 103 million rural households have access to regular savings though 7.96 million SHGs linked to banks. The number of SHGs maintaining savings accounts with banks recorded a rise in 2011-12.

Regional rural banks (RRBs) and cooperative banks form part of the Indian banking system. Government of India launched a Recapitalisation Programme in 40 of the 82 RRBs to ensure that their capital to risk-weighted assets ratio (CRAR) level reaches 9 per cent by March 2012. Of the total 82 RRBs only 15 have failed to reach the stipulated level. During 2011-12, 79 of the total were able to make profits: net profit rose to ₹ 20 billion from the previous year's level of ₹ 17 billion. RRBs have also been involved in the strategy for financial inclusion. RRBs have a network of 16,914 branches and they are expected to open another 1,700 branches during 2012-13.

The cooperative sector has two arms, the urban cooperative sector and the rural cooperative sector. The financial health of the urban cooperative sector has shown some improvement in more recent years; 61 per cent of the urban cooperative banks (UCBs) which account for 78 per cent of the total banking business of the UCB sector, had credit ratings of 'A' and 'B' reflecting good financial health. The rural cooperative sector comprises 31 state cooperative banks (StCBs), 370 district central cooperative banks (DCCBs) and 93,413 primary agricultural credit societies (PACS). StCBs and District Central Cooperative Banks (DCCBs) showed some improvements in profitability and asset quality, attributable in part to the implementation of the revival package for short-term rural cooperative sector. This is in sharp contrast to the continuous increase in losses recorded by these cooperatives in years before 2008-09. Going forward, commercial banks will have to walk the road map set for Basel III implementation. It may be recalled that the

Basel Committee on Banking Supervision (BCBs) issued in December 2010 a comprehensive reform package entitled: "Basel III: A Global Regulatory Framework for More Resilient Banks and Banking Systems." The objective of the reform package is to improve the banking sector's ability to absorb shocks arising from financial and economic stress, and thereby reduce the risk of spillover from financial sector to the real economy. Consequently RBI issued final guidelines on Basel III implementation by Indian banks. The key features of the guidelines are: first total capital must be at least 9 per cent of risk-weighted assets (RWAs). Second, in addition, the Capital Conservation Buffer (CCB) in the form of common equity of 2.5 per cent of RWAs is required to be maintained. Third, a low-risk-based Tier-I leverage has been prescribed. The implementation period of Basel III capital requirements including CCB and regulatory deductions will begin from January 1, 2013 and will be fully implemented by March 31, 2018. So far as public sector banks (PSBs) are concerned Government of India is committed to adequately capitalise them.

Overall, in addition to the strengthening of their capital base, banks would need to focus on strengthening their credit appraisal and post-sanction loan monitoring system to minimise NPAs, make financial inclusion more meaningful and revisit lending to priority sectors.

36

Rejuvenating the Cooperative Sector

IN the current discussions on economic reforms, we do not seem to have paid adequate attention to the development of the co-operative sector. In the late 1950s, we had great expectations from the cooperatives not only in respect of credit but also in other areas like linking production with marketing of agricultural commodities. Cooperatives as an institution bless both the producer and the consumer and hence building up of co-operatives was viewed in the larger context of evolving a counter-veiling force against capitalism, particularly predatory capitalism.

For instance, we have seen that in the recent bout of food inflation, it was the middleman (trader) who raised the prices artificially and exploited both the consumer and producer: this phenomenon was conspicuous in the case of fruits and vegetables. The enthusiasm to build the cooperatives sector generated by the recommendations of All-India Rural Credit Survey, 1956, did result in some success stories but it waned subsequently. The cooperative movement lost its plan. Today where are the committed leaders like Vaikunth Lal Mehta or Prof D.R. Gadgil? The intellectual leadership to guide the cooperative movement seems to have evaporated. Today, when our policy makers think of prices of food articles, their focus seems to be more on permitting foreign direct investment (FDI) in retail than on streamlining agricultural marketing arrangements at the grass roots. Official economists are talking in terms of FDI retail as an instrument of control for food inflation! The success stories of cooperative development, dairying in Anand in Gujarat, or Warana in Maharashtra, or cooperative sugar factories in Maharashtra demonstrate concretely how these have benefited both the producer and the consumer and have led to the healthy growth of the industry concerned. In the context of macroeconomic development of the Indian economy, there is merit in seeking to enlarge the share of the cooperative sector. The All-India Rural Credit Survey Report began by stating: "Cooperation has failed: but cooperation must succeed." Is it time now to repeat the slogan? The point is cooperative development should be an integral part of economic reforms.

Cooperative Credit Institutions

India has been a pioneer in promoting the cooperative banking and allied institutions, because these play an important role in financing agriculture and allied activities, small-scale industries, micro enterprises and self-employed workers. In the initial stages, the cooperative movement evolved as a voluntary movement but in the aftermath of the recommendations of All-India Rural Credit Survey 1956, the movement entered into a state-partnered phase. Its subsequent growth was rapid. Let us look at the share of cooperative institutions in the total flow of institutional credit. The broad dimensions are as follows: total flows: ₹ 225,000 crore; commercial banks ₹ 1,57,000 crore, cooperatives ₹ 44,000 crore and regional rural banks (RRBs) ₹ 25,000 crore (2007-08). Thus about 20 per cent of total institutional credit is accounted for by cooperatives.

Perhaps a more important feature of cooperative development is that the penetrative outreach of the command area of the rural cooperative is formidable as emphasised by V.K. Sharma (see RBI Bulletin January 2012). Commercial banks and RRBs account for some 33,000 rural branches. In sharp contrast, the network of co-operative credit institutions accounts for a total of 1,22,590 service centres: 33 state cooperative banks with 953 branches; 371 district central cooperative banks (DCCBs) with 12,858 branches; and 109,000 primary agricultural credit societies (PACS).

Thus although in terms of magnitudes of flow of credit, the role of co-operative credit institutions is somewhat modest, the ubiquitous presence of these institutions is quite obvious. This has great relevance for financial inclusion. Unfortunately, Reserve Bank of India (RBI) seems to think that financial inclusion is the exclusive prerogative of commercial banks. There is a need to involve cooperative credit institutions in this exercise. In fact, RBI's permission to PACS to act as Business Correspondents is tantamount to de-emphasise the role of PACS. Instead RBI should think in terms of strengthening PACS so that they can act as banks in their own right.

One way of strengthening PACS and other cooperative credit institutions is to link them with commercial banks on the lines of the NABARD scheme—Self-Help Groups (SHGs) and Banks Linkage programme. This scheme has proved to be very successful and there is no reason why the PAC-Bank linkages should not. We could pursue such programmes.

RBI and Cooperatives

As is well known, NABARD supervises the cooperative credit institutions and RBI regulates them. Has this bifurcation of functions led to RBI distancing itself from the cooperative sector? One begins to wonder.

For instance, take the recent developments in RRBs. They were not in a good shape. RBI went on restructuring and amalgamation of RRBs: their number was reduced from 196 in early 2000s to only 82. Many of them were recapitalised. As a result the net profits of RRBs have recorded an increase in recent years. Even the RRB in Bihar has produced handsome profits.

Why not a similar exercise for the net-work of cooperative financial institutions? Of course, following the recommendations of the Vaidyanathan Committee Government of India has decided to provide massive financial assistance of some ₹ 19,330 crore to the short-term cooperative credit structure. This is indeed welcome, but not enough. RBI should take a proactive interest in development of cooperatives, as does it in the case of public sector banks.

A number of elected boards of cooperative institutions are under super session. At the end of March 2010, a total of 1,118 were under super session including state cooperative banks (StCBs), DCCBs, State Cooperative Agriculture and Rural Development Bank (SCARDB) and Primary Cooperative Agriculture and Rural Development Bank (PCARDB). These need to be revived.

RBI must cease to think of cooperatives not merely as a channel—second class channel at that—of credit delivery, although this is an important function. They must be inspired by the larger vision of building up the cooperative sector as a counter-veiling power to private trade. Cooperatives must take on other allied functions like food processing and storage, transport, marketing and agricultural research and extension. Such concerted efforts alone can make the cooperative sector vibrant, and benefit both the producer and the consumer.

IV

Fiscal Policy

37

Budgets: Underlying Economic Philosophy

ALTHOUGH the presentation of the budgets is an annual affair, one should judge an individual budget not in isolation but as part of a continuum: say for five years coinciding with a Five Year Plan or the tenure of a Government. In fact the measures announced in these budgets should be inspired by the underlying economic philosophy. Only such an approach can produce good outcome. Let us look at the speech of Finance Minister Pranab Mukherjee presenting the 2012-13 budget proposals. Three specific measures may be discussed: import of gold, capital market and commercial banks and foreign direct investment (FDI) in retail.

These measures suggest there is no continuity or consistency in the budget proposals because they are not informed by any economic philosophy, *ad hocism* is writ large on them. Second, our policy-makers are obsessed with imitating the developed countries. Third, India-specific issues are not factored into these measures. For instance, nowhere is there an explanation of the rationale for liberalisation of gold imports. Why was the magnitude of imports allowed to assume alarming proportions? Even now the Finance Minister mentions only the impact of gold imports on current account deficits and not their unproductive nature. Why are our policy-makers obsessed with promoting the capital market? In India public sector banks (PSBs) play as much an important role as capital market, in promoting growth, particularly inclusive growth. Why is income from interest on bank deposits not exempted from tax as is dividend income? Our policy-makers, also appear to be swayed over by current fashions in economic thinking: example promoting FDI in retail trade.

Import of Gold

To quote the Finance Minister: "One of the primary drivers of the current account deficit has been the growth of almost 50 per cent in imports of gold and other precious metals in the first three quarters of this year. I have been advised to strengthen steps already taken to check this trend for better results. I propose to increase basic customs duty on standard gold bars: gold coins of purity exceeding 99.5 per cent and platinum from 2 per cent to 4 per cent and on non-standard gold from 5 per cent to 10 per cent.

During the first phase of economic reforms in the 1990s one of the most retrogressive measures introduced was the liberalisation of import of gold. The annual average level of imports of gold worked out to $5 billion in the initial years. Import of gold is in a way definancialisation of savings: because financial savings which could have been channeled to productive purposes would be diverted to unproductive investment in gold. Today, in metropolitan and bigger towns there are more jewellery shops than grocery shops. Surely, the World Trade Organization (WTO) did not prescribe the liberalisation of gold imports. Even public sector banks are encouraged to sell gold coins. This is a clear case of perversion of priorities in development. Nobody would, of course, advocate a total ban on import of gold but what is required is restraint on the magnitude of imports. At last the Finance Minister has discovered this truth after a decade! One hopes that he would not stop at this measure.

Capital Market and Banks

To boost the capital market, the budget introduces a new scheme: "To encourage the flow of savings in financial instruments and improve the depth of domestic capital market, it is proposed to introduce a new scheme. The scheme would allow for IT deduction of 50 per cent to new retail investors who invest upto ₹ 50,000 directly in equities and whose annual income is below ₹ 10 lakh. The scheme will have a lock-in-period of 3 years."

This is again a hangover of the efforts to provide artificial incentives to promote capital market—a policy pursued during the reform period of the 1990s. We must now remember that capital markets the world over are no longer the barometers of economic activity. Nor does the contribution of capital markets to capital formation of the corporate sector significant. The bulk of the capital formation of the corporate sector is accounted for by internal generation of resources. Our policy-makers' obsession to develop the capital market should be tempered by ground realities. There is an India-specific reason why we should not discriminate against public sector banks. While dividend income is totally exempt from tax, interest income from deposits with banks is subject to tax. What needs to be underlined is that public sector undertaking (PSU) banks provide 40 per cent of their total lending to priority sectors—sectors which have no access to capital market. Thus the contribution of PSU banks to the growth of the economy is as important as that of the capital market. The tax regime should not therefore discriminate against banks. There should be a level playing field for both. Thus the proposal in the budget "to allow individual taxpayers, a deduction of upto ₹ 10,000 for interest from savings bank accounts" is a poor consolation. Interest income from bank deposits should be treated on par with dividend income.

FDI in Retail

It has become fashionable to argue that FDI in retail has emerged as an instrument of inflation control, after the Chief Economic Adviser made a statement to that effect. The Finance Minister states "Organised retail helps in reducing cost of intermediation due to economies of scale, benefiting both consumers and producers. At present, FDI in single brand and in cash and carry wholesale trade is permitted to the extent of 100 per cent. The decision in respect of allowing FDI in multi-brand retail trade upto 51 per cent, subject to compliance with specified conditions, has been held in abeyance. Efforts are on to arrive at a broad-based consensus in consultation with State Governments."

The new enthusiasm of our policy-makers for permitting FDI in retail is comparable to the obsession to policy-makers to develop the capital market, referred to above. Both must be viewed in a proper perspective.

The point is RBI's record in managing inflation is excellent. In fact recently *The Economist* complimented RBI for its past performance: "Judging by the numbers, RBI is among the world's best central banks. Its record on balancing growth and inflation is decent enough. Since 1995 whole sale prices have risen by an average of 6 per cent per year, not too far from RBI's comfort of 5 per cent. Growth has averaged 7 per cent per year". RBI therefore does not have to seek shelter under the unknown quantity of FDI in retail acting as an anti-inflationary instrument. Moreover, the benefits of organised retail can be reaped by Indian capital as well. Anand Dairy is a concrete example. The point is that if you want to justify FDI in retail, by all means do so with other reasons and not as an anti-inflationary measure.

38

Economic Survey

Erudition and Policy Making

THE *Economic Survey* issued annually by the Government of India, Ministry of Finance, remains an authoritative document on the state of the Indian economy. One aspect of the document which has not received adequate attention of the analysts is that during the last couple of years, there are attempts to make the document more erudite or scholarly. For instance, the cover page of the *Economic Survey 2011-12* contains the Phillips Curve portraying the relationship between inflation and unemployment. As most of us are aware, such relationship is directly relevant to developed economies, rather than to the Indian economy characterised by large-scale underemployment and disguised unemployment. The point is that such erudition may sometimes aid but is not a substitute for sensible policy-making. Policy-making in a country or under specific circumstances is essentially an art which cannot be encapsuled in an unique formula or theoretical construct.

Let us elaborate. The Ministry of Finance, Government of India, organised in December 2011, a series of lectures, seminars and workshops. The week was declared as the Delhi Economics Conclave on the theme 'Economic Policies for Emerging Economies'. The conclave brought together eminent economic thought leaders, economic practitioners as well as policy-makers. More than 400 participants from diverse countries including the US, UK, Germany, Australia, Singapore and Bangladesh attended. The deliberations converged on the view that emerging economies need to have strong back-up plans and focus more on South-South trade. Six priorities for India were identified: investment and capital formation; increased agricultural output and productivity through government investment; fiscal consolidation: education and skill development to harness demographic dividend; ensure the flow of foreign investment for asset creation; and focus on inclusive growth through improved health facilities, education and financial inclusions.

So far so good. Such exchange of ideas and empirical experience does help us in formulating our policies. But only up to a point. The Commission on Growth and Development sponsored by the World Bank (WB) which submitted its report in 2008 came to the conclusion that there is no generic formula for growth. "Each country has specific characteristics and historical experiences that must be reflected in its growth story". It is here that skills of sensible policy-making in the country-specific context are tested.

Let us take one more example of erudition that the *Economic Survey* seeks to impose on monetary policy-makers . "Our understanding of the empirical foundations of monetary policy has undergone a virtual paradigm shift with the arrival of, a new statistical tool, victor autoregression (VAR) developed by Christopher Sims... By using this technique, researcher have been able to tease out the causal links between macro economic policy variables and inflation...." After a couple of paragraphs, the survey adds: "Unfortunately, most of these studies are based on US or European experience". If the survey itself is fully conscious of the serious limitations of the applicability of this technique to the Indian situation; the discussion of the issue becomes merely an academic exercise. Recently the Reserve Bank of India (RBI) has been applauded for its skills in balancing growth with inflation. What will the RBI do with such an unusable instrument?

Take another example of Economic Survey's discourse on Values and Economics: "There is research in psychology and evolutionary biology which shows that morality, altruism and other regarding values are an innate part of the human mind even though the social setting in which a person lives can nurture or stunt these traits.... There was the celebrated work of Fukuyama, which illustrated how societies that managed to develop higher levels of trust worthiness among the people were societies that had achieved grater economic prosperity." As a philosophical proposition such quotations are indeed welcome. But what is their relevance for policy formulation? The *Economic Survey* is in context with merely quoting the above propositions.

It would have been useful if, for instance, the *Economic Survey* had sought to derive some lessons from this discussion for the current campaign in India against widespread corruption.

The same reluctance to analyse the applicability of general principles to India-specific issued is evident on other crucial issues. The most conspicuous example relates to import of gold. "Gold and silver imports of US $ 50 billion grew by 46.2 per cent" during the period April-January 2011-12. This is all that the survey states. Why have these imports grown to this alarming figure from merely US$ 5 billion in early 2000s? What are the implications for balance of payments in particular and economic growth in general? The *Economic Survey* is totally silent on the issues: it is the Finance Minister to whom the credit for spelling out the implications should go. To quote from his budget speech: "One of the primary drivers of the current account deficit has been the growth of almost 50 per cent in imports of gold and other precious metals in the first three quarters of this year. I have been advised to strengthen steps already taken to check this trend for better results, I propose to increase basic customs duty on standard gold bars: gold coins of purity exceeding 99.5 per cent and platinum from 2 per cent to 4 per cent and on non-standard gold from 5 per cent to 10 per cent".

Even the Finance Minister has only touched the fringe of the problem. Import of gold is in a way definancialisation of savings: because financial savings which could have been channeled to productive purposes have been directed to unproductive investment in gold. A poor country like India cannot afford to fritter away its savings into unproductive assets like gold. It is tentamount to perversion of development priorities. We should never have allowed gold imports to soar to US$ 50 billion from the level of only US$ 5 billion. From this point of view, the step taken by Finance Minister is only a baby step. He should take drastic steps to contain gold imports. On such a critical issue the *Economic Survey* is silent.

The other critical issue on which *Economic Survey* could have focused is food inflation. Apart from making appropriate noises that foreign direct investment (FDI) in retail would help in containing inflation, the survey does not make any other recommendations. Two issues are relevant here. In the case of fruits and vegetables, which have contributed greatly to food inflation, the middlemen's margins are very high. The question is to streamline marketing arrangements. Secondly, we have substantial stocks of foodgrains: at end of January 2012, 26 million tonnes of wheat, and 55 million tonnes of rice. We can moderate the rise in open market prices of rice and wheat through the operations of Food Corporation of India (FCI) which can emerge and market maker.

Discourses on economic theory are welcome but documents like the *Economic Survey* would do well to focus on issues of sensible policy-making.

V

Food Security

39

Total Food Security

An Alternative Model

THE National Food Security Bill (NFSB), awaiting the approval of Parliament, seeks to provide total 'food security' to the bulk of the population, say 70-78 per cent. The word 'total' is true in another sense. The basic approach is to ensure home delivery, as it were, of a specified quantum of subsidised foodgrains—doorstep delivery of PDS (public distribution system) grains is the wording in the draft bill. Although there has been a lot of discussion on the modalities of the bill, the basic philosophy underlying the approach is never spelt out. "There are compelling economic, social, political and ethical imperatives for such legal guarantee of protection from hunger."

Although the objective of the bill is indeed laudable, the proposed *modus operandi* of achieving the objective is, to say the least, clumsy. The hazards of operationalising the proposed alternative are so forbidding that they may result in logistic disaster as we will discuss presently. Even in the most advanced welfare states, direct provision of food is rarely resorted to. Establishing soup kitchens to protect the homeless destitutes during the winter is the nearest programme we can think of. But this is marginal and not central to the objective of providing total food security. The developed countries may provide social security or unemployment dole, enabling the unemployed to access food.

Our policy-makers' quest for home delivery of food—if not cooked food, foodgrains—to the bulk of the population is thus ill—conceived in theory and not implementable in practice. The essential ingredients of a workable model of total food security are three. First, the state should take care—and take care directly—of the vulnerable sections of the population. We have already designed such scheme: the mid-day meal programme for school children covering some 15 crore children, and the Integrated Child Development Services (ICDS) to promote nutritional supplement to children up to the age of six. Here the states' involvement in providing directly food or foodgrains to these sections is justified. Of course, such food is highly subsidised or sometime totally free.

Second, schemes 'enabling' economic access to food: The Mahatma Gandhi National Rural Employment Guarantee Act (NREGA) is a concrete example of this approach. The Act guarantees 100 days of employment in a year to an adult in every rural household. Today about 5 crore rural households are benefiting from this programme, which takes care of the food security of this section of rural labour.

Third, if we are planning to offer food access to some sections through the open market—as in the case of rural labour mentioned above—we must ensure that food prices in the open market are steady or nearly steady. Fortunately, we have the institutional mechanism to ensure a steady price regime at least in the case of rice and wheat.

The broad economic philosophy underlying this alternative model of ensuring total food security is thus clear. Catering to the requirements of the vulnerable sections of the population is the direct responsibility of the state. For the rest of the population, the states should create an 'enabling environment' in the sense they are able to fend for themselves, without the state requiring to spoon-feed them, as it were. The enunciation of these principles also exposes another major conceptual flaw in the model of the National Food Security Bill. Why should we cover 70 per cent of the population? Are we assuming that 70 per cent of the population which we propose to support by subsidised foodgrains will remain hovering around or just above the poverty line? This assumption militates against the development objective of reducing poverty or at least reducing the size of population eligible for subsidy. On the one hand, we complain about the high levels of food subsidies and on the other we propose to subsidise perpetually undeserving sections of the population!

Market Intervention by Food Corporation of India

One of the essential conditions of the success of 'the enabling method' is that open market prices of foodgrains should be stable.

Fortunately, the Food Corporation of India (FCI) with its massive stocks of rice and wheat has emerged as a counter-veiling force to private trade in respect of rice and wheat. It should therefore function as a market maker in respect of rice and wheat, by unloading its stocks in appropriate quantities in pockets where price shows a tendency to rise. It should thus be possible to ensure a stable level of prices of rice and wheat in the open market. We have been treating FCI as a glorified godown keeper and this must change.

Let us now turn to the hazards of implementing the proposals of the National Food Security Bill.

Hazards of Implementation

First, the scheme involves a quantum jump in procurement and storage of foodgrains. Procurement of some 60 to 65 million tonnes as against the present level of some 54 million tonnes. This is again on the assumption of being able to achieve higher levels of production—an aspect on which the bill does not offer any concrete proposals.

Second, this imposes additional burden on the PDS. As it is, PDS is in a tottering condition. There are 'leakages' due to corruption, transport losses and losses due to spoilage. The TV channels have shown recently how the grain is allowed to rot exposed to rain, or rats are eating away the grains from the godowns of FCI. It is thus clear that unless these deficiencies are rectified, it would not be prudent to entrust PDS with greater responsibilities.

Third, the massive increase in food subsidy, say from the present level of some ₹ 56,000 crore to something more than ₹ 70,000 crore. The budget deficit which might reach 5.5 per cent of gross domestic product (GDP) in 2011-12 is already beyond the comfort levels and how can we hope to cope with larger food subsidy?

Finally, apart from financial implications, the massive increase in procurement, storage and distribution of foodgrains might pose problems of managerial and administrative bottleneck.

On the whole, the 'enabling method', that is the state creating an enabling environment in which the bulk of the population can earn its 'livelihood' seems to offer a more practical alternative to the state taking upon itself the responsibility of 'directly feeding' the population with subsidised foodgrains.

40

Hunger, Poverty and Wellness of People

ALTHOUGH there is a good deal of discussion on the Food Security Bill, especially on its weaknesses, there does not seem to be an adequate appreciation of the overall context in which this bill needs to be judged. We take pride in the fact that India is the second fastest growing economy in the world but tend to forget that India continues to be the abode of the largest number of underfed and undernourished. Recently, the Prime Minister called such malnutrition 'a national shame' and added India cannot hope for a healthy future with 42 per cent of its kids below 5 years being underweight. We seem to have overlooked the fact that human indicators like adequate nutrition, basic education and health are as important as growth per se, for the wellness of people. As Amartya Sen has pointed out that even a poorer country like Bangladesh has overtaken us in terms of human development indicators like longevity, infant mortality and female literacy. Is India obsessed with growth at the cost of human development? Ideally, the problem of hunger can be tackled through elimination of poverty, higher GDP growth, employment expansion and so on. This is conventional wisdom. But this process is a long haul and may take decades. For instance, even after six decades of development planning, about 25 to 30 per cent of the population continues to be poor. However, without waiting for decades, the hunger can be solved because we have nearly adequate supply of foodgrains to feed the population. Analytically this is an important step towards evolving what might be described as 'the second best solution' eliminate hunger first, poverty later. The Food Bill is based on this premise.

While there cannot be any two opinions on the bill's basic objectives, the challenges involved in operationalising the bill are so forbidding that it may invite logistics disaster. Hence is there any alternative pragmatic route which can achieve the same end-objective? This is the question we have to pose.

Let us enumerate the challenger. First, the larger coverage of the population of say 70 per cent. Is this feasible? Second, is the larger procurement of foodgrains of say, 60 to 65 mt and their appropriate storage practicable? Third, the subsidy implications: subsidy will jump from ₹ 56,700 to ₹ 71,000 crore. Is this sustainable in the medium term?

As it is, we know that the public distribution system (PDS) is tottering. Researchers have found concrete evidence of corruption. Estimates of diversion of grains from PDS include leakages due to corruption, transport losses, and losses due to spoilage. The situation has deteriorated between 1990-2000 and 2007-08. At the beginning of the period 24 per cent of the grain was diverted. In 2007-08, 44 per cent was diverted. A TV channel has shown graphic images of FCI godowns allowing grain to rot in the open storage or of rats eating away foodgrains from godowns. How can we impose such additional burden of massive procurement, storage and distribution on a sick body?

Moreover, the whole exercise is build upon the grand assumption of acceleration of farm growth. The compound agricultural growth rate was lower than the modest targeted growth rate 4 per cent for 1991-92 of 2009-10. In the reforms period, the growth rate as a ratio of GDP growth rate decelerated from 0.61 to 0.43.

More basically, there is a logical flaw in intending to cover a larger number of say, 70 per cent of total households. Are we then assuming that a larger proportion of households would continue to remain poor to be eligible for subsidised grains even in the medium term? This is like endorsing the biblical saying the poor are always with us.

A more pragmatic approach to eliminate hunger would be a blend of supply of subsidised or even free foodgrains with market-aided programmes designed to enable households to purchase foodgrains—through employment generation, moderating open market prices and by streamlining marketing of some items of food like fruits and vegetables.

It is necessary to first identify the vulnerable sections of the population. Here it is question of supply of subsidised or even free foodgrains. Programmes already underway like the mid-day meals and child nutrition programmes should be strengthened. Besides, through a system of grant, community kitchens should be organised for the needy.

In the case of fruits and vegetables which contributed to food inflation recently, market arrangements should be streamlined. Dairy industry in Anand is a model here. The idea is to increase the share in the consumer rupee of the small producer, by cutting down large margins of the unscrupulous traders.

About the open market prices of foodgrains, here the question is one of moderating the prices of rice and wheat. Fortunately, FCI with its enormous stocks could emerge as a market maker. It could download adequate quantities of rice or wheat in the open market and ensure that open market prices of these commodities do not rise unduly.

The underlying idea is to make the open market more friendly to the low income households with the help of programmes like National Rural Employment Gurantee Act (NREGA). We are generating additional income amongst the poor so that they may be able to purchase foodgrains from the open market. Even subsidised foodgrains need to be purchased.

Thus the food supply to the vulnerable sections is the exclusive responsibility of the public sector. Even 100 per cent subsidy may be involved. To the rest of the population, our objective should be to evolve a friendly open market which provides economic access to food.

This approach is more pragmatic and does away with the monolithic organisation required by the bill. It is workable on the ground level, and would not strain the administrative and managerial skills of development administration commands.

41

A Sort of Food Utopia

RECENTLY, a group of eminent academic economists—incidentally a majority of them Indian economists based in American Universities—wrote to Sonia Gandhi saying that the proposed National Food Security (NFS) Act is "of profound importance to India's economy". But a more important part of their recommendation which deserves to be discussed is the following: "We urge you to draft The National Food Security Act in a way that would (1) provide an entitlement to a fixed basket of food or its monetary equivalent to all but the richest individuals, and (2) permit alternatives to public distribution system for delivering this entitlement. The method of delivering the subsidy should be left open to change as the available technology and the associated infrastructure change."

This is a timely warning because at present a sense of supreme complacency and total disregard for ground realities seem to characterise the approach to the authors of the National Food Security Bill (February 21, 2011) and Food Minister K.V. Thomas. Between themselves they seem to have created a sort of 'food utopia'. The basic approach of home delivery, as it were, of a specified quantum of subsidised food grains 'doorstep delivery of PDS grains' is the wording in the draft Bill, is flawed. We know that many poor households do not use the public delivery system (PDS) even when they have the necessary entitlement. Even subsidised food grains need to be purchased. Enabling the poor to purchase subsidised food grains is far more important than mere legal entitlement. We therefore have to adopt a holistic approach to ensure food security.

Basically, the National Advisory Council (NAC) recommends a much higher coverage of the population to subsidised food. Individual food entitlements proposed by NAC are: priority category 7 kgs per month and general category 5 kgs per month. It recommends a larger coverage of 72 per cent of the total population in the first phase and

78 per cent in the final phase. In the first phase, NAC estimates a total PDS requirement of 49.4 million tonnes. If we add non-PDS food grains requirements for schemes like the mid-day meals and Integrated Child Development Services (ICDS), total requirement works out to some 58 million tonnes. The NAC feels that procurement of some 60 to 65 million tonnes of food grains annually 'should not be difficult'. In 2009-10 for instance, procurement of rice and wheat was around 54 million tonnes. The subsidy implication of NAC proposals are that the total subsidy would jump from the present level of ₹ 56,700 crore to ₹ 71,837 crore.

Apart from financial implications, such larger procurement and distribution of rice and wheat pose problems of logistic disaster. As it is, PDS is in a tottering condition. How does one go about increasing production and strengthening PDS? Here NACs explanatory note merely lists a bunch of good intentions. There is no agenda for action. For instance, "There is a large potential for higher foodgrain production. India has vast untapped production reservoir in most farming systems, even with the currently available technologies."

Regarding storage of food grains in the light of the recent criticism of insensitivity of Food Corporation of India (FCI) to wastage of food grains through inappropriate storage the NAC merely states: "Urgent efforts are needed to expand, improve and modernise storage of food grains in the country...." NAC also advocates "urgent reform of PDS."

Where do these homilies lead us? Recent researchers have provided concrete evidence of corruption in the PDS. Estimates of diversion of grains from PDS include leakages due to corruption, transport losses and losses due to spoilage. Reetika Khera has shown that the situation has deteriorated between 1990-2000 and 2007-08. At the beginning of the period 24 per cent of the grain was diverted. In 2004-05, 54 per cent of the grains was diverted. At the end of 2007-08, 44 per cent of the grain was diverted. Although there are interstate differentials, this was the picture at the all-India level. There were seven major states whose performance was excellent, in the sense of negligible diversion. We cannot therefore label the PDS as 'dysfunctional' (see "Trends in Diversion of Grain from the Public Distribution System". *Economic & Political Weekly*, May 21-27, 2011). One thing is quite clear. Unless this deficiency is rectified, if would not be prudent to entrust PDS with greater responsibilities.

In the face of such evidence Food Minister is complacent about FCI. In a recent interview to a financial paper he said: "But the key thing is that the machinery has to be equipped. Compared to earlier periods, the recruitment to FCI has risen by 10 per cent. We have modernised FCI godowns through computerisation. Sitting in my office, I know the quantity, quality and distribution of grain from each godown. We have put CCTV cameras to watch operations" (*Economic Times*, June 1, 2011). If the picture is so rosy, one may ask: why did the Supreme Court ask the Government of India to distribute the grains free of cost to the poor, instead of allowing it to rot in the open storage of FCI? It is to the credit of NDTV, that they showed a couple of godowns of FCI where the grain was allowed to rot exposed to rain, or rats were eating away grains from one such godown. The point is that much needs to be done to improve the storage of grains in the godowns of FCI.

Earlier, I had occasion to point out that the basic approach of NAC to food security is flawed. Providing food security does not mean that Government should produce and deliver a stipulated quantity of food grains at subsidised prices to targeted households, as the NAC proposals seem to suggest. The magnitudes involved in such operations are so forbidding that it may result in logistic disaster. What is required is creating an environment which enables households to purchase food grains through employment generation, moderating open market prices of rice and wheat, and by streamlining marketing arrangements of some items like fruits and vegetables. If public sector banks (PSBs) can use business correspondent (BC) model there is no reason why FCI cannot use private trade to reach targeted households. Private and public sector participation should be an essential ingredient of a well-designed food security model. Protecting the vulnerable sections of the population through say mid-day meals or child nutrition programmes would, of course, continue to be the exclusive responsibility of public sector institutions.

42

Man-made Food Grains' Mountain

IN the normal course, one thinks in terms of the spectre of drought or food scarcity looming in the horizon. Today, it is different. The spectre of foodgrains mountain is haunting us. The situation is so desperate that Dr Ashok Gulati, Chairman of the Commission for Agricultural Costs and Prices—very much part of the establishment—is driven to come out openly to issue the warning to Government as follows: With the bumper harvest, India will have a record foodgrains stocks of 75 million tonnes by end June 2012, when wheat procurement operations would be practically over. Unfortunately, our storage is woefully inadequate to accommodate such large stocks. The Food Corporation of India (FCI) however has a covered storage capacity of some 31 million tonnes while state Agencies/SWCs (State Warehousing Corporations) have covered capacity of some 15 million tonnes which is being used for storage capacity for central foodgrains stocks. Thus the total covered storage capacity for central foodgrains stocks is lower than 50 million tonnes. Thus about one-third of total stocks would have to be stored in the open and therefore would be vulnerable to damages, especially during the monsoon.

TV channels have exposed how FCI mismanages its food stocks: by allowing the grains to rot during rains or by allowing rats to eat away part of the stocks. Dr Gulati's warning is therefore timely. Dr Gulati has offered several options of how best we can productively utilise these foodgrains.

Fortunately, one option he has not mentioned is large scale export of foodgrains. It is necessary to highlight this point because this is what our policy-makers did in the early 2000s. The most disturbing aspect of food management was that India chose to export a huge quantity of 27 million tonnes of rice and wheat during the three consecutive years—2001-02 to 2003-04. During this phase our policy-makers were intoxicated with the market theology. They wanted to cut down food subsidy drastically. The poor must fend for themselves. They not only raised the issue price of foodgrains but also tightened the conditions of access to public sector foodgrains. The net result was that offtake of foodgrains from the public distribution system (PDS) declined. There was thus a policy-induced build-up of foodgrains stocks upto 60 million tonnes. No wonder our policy-makers sought the soft option of exporting foodgrains for tackling the so-called 'surplus foodgrains' problem. This was nothing short of development atrocity when viewed against the background of India being the abode of the largest number of underfed and undernourished persons in the world. What is worse, the same policy-makers who shunned subsidy for domestic consumption of foodgrains had no qualms about subsidising export of foodgrains. I have earlier written that if Mahatma Gandhi were alive, he would have organised a *satyagraha* against such mindless pursuit of foodgrains management policy.

Our contemporary policy-makers are, of course, more sensitive to food security issues and in fact are moving towards more ambitious food security bill which involves larger procurement and distribution of foodgrains. Of course, it has its own problems. The point is that the export lobby is quite strong and our policy-makers would do well to remain uninfluenced by it.

The situation has also exposed the 'commitment deficit' of policy-makers. We have been discussing the need to build adequate storage facilities not only for foodgrains but also for other agricultural commodities since the recommendations of the All-India Rural Credit Survey in 1956. We have resources to finance massive imports of gold annually to the tune of $50 billion but no money to build storage facilities for such critical commodities like foodgrains.

The spectre of foodgrains mountain can also be looked upon as a god-sent opportunity to take a second look at the basic approach to the proposed Food Security Act. One hopes that the framers of this act are shaken out of their sense of supreme complacency. I have written earlier that the magnitudes involved in procurement, storage and distribution of foodgrains, are so formidable that the proposal is likely to prove a logistic disaster. As it is, the PDS is tottering, with its 'leakages' which are now well documented. We do not have the storage capacity and food administration is far from efficient. Where then do we go from here? This crisis also exposes our unpreparedness to effectively implement the proposed Food Security Act.

A deeper reflection on the issue reveals that mandating PDS to deliver at the doorsteps of the bulk of the population subsidised foodgrains is neither desirable nor practical. There are more efficient ways to achieve the same end-objective. Briefly, let us retain the core of the present PDS: streamline it, plug the leakages and improve managerial efficiency. Around this core PDS, we should build other institutional mechanisms which would use foodgrains directly. For instance, we do already have such programmes: mid-day meal scheme providing cooked meals to school children and Integrated Child Development Services (ICD) to promote nutritional supplement to children up to the age of six. The mid-day meal programme covers some 15 crore children. We should widen the scope of such programmes. Such programmes do not cast any burden on PDS: nor do they need storage facilities.

The Mahatma Gandhi National Rural Employment Guarantee Act (MGNREGA) holds out great potential for use of foodgrains directly perhaps as part of wages to be paid in kind. At present this scheme provides employment to 5.5 crore households. Two impressive features of the scheme may be highlighted. First, the share of women in the total employment is 48 per cent. Second, the share of water conservation works in the total projects undertaken under the scheme is 48 per cent. There is enormous scope for extending the scheme. A recent World Bank (WB) evaluation of the scheme has all appreciation for the project: "The scheme also tries to address some causes of poverty in rural India. By its "bottom-up" demand-driven nature, it aims to empower the rural poor to help them take serious actions in various domains that help them escape poverty" (Does India's Employment Guarantee Scheme guarantee employment? March 2012).

A Monolithic organisation mandated to deliver subsidised foodgrains to the bulk of the population is perhaps not a practical proposition. Around the core PDS, we should build a number of small institutions catering to different segments which can make use of foodgrains directly.

43

High Food Prices Erode Purchasing Power

INTERNATIONAL food prices remained largely stable through the first half of 2010 but they started surging during the second half of 2010 and have continued to rise in the current year. In January 2011, the benchmark index for food prices of the FAO (Food and Agriculture Organization) exceeded the steepest price level on record in 2008. In February 2011, global food prices recorded a rise of 30 per cent on year-on-year basis. As in the case of the 2007-08 episode, rising global food prices are getting transmitted into higher domestic food prices in the developing Asian economies. Rising food prices pose important macroeconomic policy challenges particularly in emerging economies, because of their impact on inflation and poverty reduction.

Control of food prices remains intrinsically important for control of inflation. But if we realise the adverse impact that high food prices have on the incidence of poverty, this adds a new dimension to the role of food prices on poverty reduction. Apart from the useful analytical insights this approach provides, it is relevant for macroeconomic policy. Understanding this phenomenon is important, because according to Asian Development Bank's (ADB) assessment, the near-term outlook for international food prices is that they will continue to rule high and also will be volatile.

The ADB in its recent Report on Global Food Price Inflation and Developing Asia (March 2011) has raised some critical issues for macroeconomic management of food and these do not seem to have received adequate attention by Indian policy-makers. We seem to be carried away by the more grandiloquent schemes like the proposed Food Security Act which promises to 'home-deliver', as it were, a certain quantum of subsidised food grains to a broadly defined, poverty groups. The more urgent issues raised by ADB need to be addressed immediately.

The most critical issue raised by ADB is: 'Higher food prices erode the purchasing power of households and undermine the recent gains from poverty reduction'. For instance, ADB estimates that a 10 per cent rise in domestic food prices in developing Asia could push an additional 64.4 million into poverty. For India, ADB estimates that a 10 per cent rise in food prices would add another 29 million persons to poverty (poverty line $1.25 a day) or an increase in poverty by some 5 percentage points.

Indian policy-makers need to reassess their approach to macro food management and perhaps re-order their priorities. We must pay more attention to micro food management. Unfortunately, more recent events have exposed how our policy-makers have become increasingly insensitive to starvation and malnutrition. The Supreme Court recently had to direct the Government of India that larger quantum of foograins be released to the poor, even free of cost, instead of allowing food grains to rot in the open storages of Food Corporation of India (FCI). Again on May 14, 2011, the Supreme Court directed the Government to release an additional one million tonnes of cereals to safeguard against starvation and malnutrition. Take another example. The Centre allocates food grains to states under the Targeted Public Distribution System (TPDS) and other welfare schemes of Government of India. Unfortunately, the offtake of food grains by states, under these schemes has always been lower, say 35 to 40 per cent of the total allocation. That is many beneficiaries do not take deliveries as per their entitlements. When we are going through lofty discourses on food security, this performance of states reflects the majestic indifference of the bureaucracy and the policy- makers towards poverty and starvation. In any case, why is not the Centre goading states to make full use of allotted quota?

It is now too well-known that primitive methods of storage of rice and wheat by the FCI result in substantial losses of food grains. We have been talking about building adequate storage and warehousing capacity since the days of the All-India Rural Credit Survey, 1956. Today, we have learnt to build 'world class' airports. But what about simple brick and mortar godowns to store our huge stocks of rice and wheat procured and built up by the FCI? We seem to have our priorities wrong. Allowing a single kilo of food grains to rot becomes a criminal act of negligence in a society which continues to be the abode of the largest number of underfed and undernourished persons in the world.

Finally, on the price policy. This new dimension, namely high food prices eroding the incomes of lower middle classes, and perhaps pushing some of them into the poor classes brings into sharp focus the critical role of open market prices of food grains. So far we have focused only on public distribution system (PDS) and on supply of subsidised food grains. Protecting the vulnerable classes is the first priority. Fortunately we have the FCI with its huge stocks of rice and wheat. These stocks are far in excess of buffer stock norms. For instance, in January 2010, we had in the Central Pool total stocks of 47.5 million tonnes of rice and wheat, against the buffer norm of 20 million tonnes. Technically, we have also an Open Market Sales Scheme. It is therefore easy to influence the open market prices of rice and wheat by unloading appropriate quantities in the open market. But so far the scheme has remained a paper tiger. FCI has never conducted major sales operations under this scheme. For instance, in 2008-09 the total offtake under the scheme was only 1.2 million tonnes. In fact these quantities include exports. It is therefore necessary to activate this scheme so that it could play a more effective role in moderating the open market prices of rice and wheat.

Overall, the main point which emerges from the discussion is that moderating the open market prices of rice and wheat should become an integral part of our food price policy. We should cease to treat the FCI as a glorified godown-keeper, as we have been doing all these years and make its operations an effective tool for moderating prices. Similarly, our indifferent attitude towards proper storage of food grains should change. Losses through inappropriate storage should be minimised. Only thus can we meet the challenge posed by high food prices to reduction of poverty.

44

Food Security *versus* Employment Security

THE proposed Food Security Act has run into difficulties. It may be recalled that the National Advisory Council (NAC) had proposed legal subsidised food entitlements for nearly 75 per cent of the country's population covering both the priority (BPL—below the poverty line) and general (APL—above the poverty line) households by 2013-14. The Rangarajan Committee which examined these recommendations has rejected the proposal because the NAC formula involves massive increase in procurement of food grains from the present level of say some 57 million tonnes of rice and wheat to say some 74 million tonnes. Further, the amount of food subsidy would go up from the present level of say ₹ 52,000 crore to ₹ 90,000 crore by 2013-14. Thus the Rangarajan Committee has stated that such massive increase in procurement and a sharp rise in subsidies is not feasible. Even apart from these substantive issues, the large distribution network with wider coverage of households, as recommended by NAC, required is simply not in place. As it is, the public distribution system (PDS) is tottering there are the so-called leakages—good quality food grains meant for PDS find their way to the open market, the BPL families to whom the PDS is supposed to cater are denied the benefits and so on. While there cannot be any two opinions on the desirability for providing subsidised food grains to larger sections of the population, on pragmatic grounds alone this NAC proposal deserves to be rejected. First reform the PDS before expanding its network and imposing additional responsibilities on it. The delivery channels of PDS are rusted: cleanse them first before thinking in terms of enlarging them.

The basic approach of the NAC seems to have missed the central point: food security does not mean home delivery as it were of a stipulated quantity of food grains to the households but it entails enabling these households to purchase these quantities from the market or PDS. Let me illustrate. Under the present arrangements allocations of food grains for BPL families are made at 35 kg per family per month for all accepted 6.52 crore BPL families in the country. Allocations for APL category is 15 kg per family per month. The Central Issue Price (CIP) is so fixed that these are highly subsidised. For instance, food subsidy has risen from ₹ 23,000 crore in 2005-06 to ₹ 51,000 crore in 2010-11.

Food security does not mean simply making larger quantity of food grains available through the PDS, although this is important. Larger quantum of food grains is a necessary, though not a sufficient condition for ensuring food security. It is also necessary to enable the households to purchase the subsidised food grains. We therefore have to adopt a holistic approach to ensure food security. Four components of such approach can be briefly outlined: increasing the production base, enlarging employment opportunities, improving the operations of Food Corporation of India (FCI) and streamlining marketing of vegetables and fruits.

Increasing substantially the level of food grains production is a pre-requisite of providing food security. Unfortunately, the per capita availability of food grains has shown, over the years, a decline though marginally. The per capita availability of food grains declined from 494 grams per day in 2001 to 444 grams in 2009. This trend needs to be reversed. Accelerating the growth of food grains production thus becomes imperative.

The only asset the poor have is labour and hence providing employment is the best means of enabling the poor to buy subsidised food grains. The National Rural Employment Guarantee Scheme (NREGS), the Central Government's work guarantee programme, has done wonders in this field. Through this programme an income of ₹ 39,100 crore was injected into 52 million households in 2009-10. Employment security is thus as important as food security. We must enlarge this scheme so that all those who seek work will get it.

The FCI was originally established as a counter-veiling force to private trade in food grains. Under private trade both the farmers and consumers were the loosers. FCI provided price support to farmers and subsidised food grains to consumers through PDS. So far so good. Over years, FCI with its elephantine structure has become incompetent and insensitive. The Supreme Court was compelled to tell the Government of India: it is better to provide free food grains to the poor, rather than allowing food grains to rot in the open storage of FCI. With its massive stocks, FCI should be able to moderate the prices of rice and wheat in the open market. Why did we allow the prices of primary articles to rise by an annual average of 9 per cent during the five years period 2005-06 to 2009-10? Because FCI is not active in its open market sales of rice and wheat. For instance, in 2009-10, open market sales of FCI were only 16 lakh tonnes of wheat and 5 lakh tonnes of rice. If open market prices of rice and wheat are moderated, it will go a long way towards promoting food security. The best way seems to be to make FCI an autonomous institution managed by an independent board consisting of economists, statisticians and marketing experts. By appropriate off-loading of its stocks, FCI would be able to moderate open market prices of food grains.

In the recent spurt in food inflation, prices of vegetables and fruits played havoc. The humble onions and brinjals claimed headlines in the daily papers. Such soaring of prices benefited neither the farmer nor the consumer but the trader. Streamlining of marketing of these products is overdue. There is no reason why we should not try to emulate the Anand experience in dairying in terms of managing the supply chain and providing remunerative prices to farmers. Today, if prices of onions rule at ₹ 15 per kg in Aurangabad, they sell at ₹ 50 in Mumbai.

Providing food security does not mean that Government should produce and deliver a stipulated quantity of food grains at subsidised prices to the targeted households, as the NAC proposals seem to suggest. It is a question of enabling households to purchase food grains, through employment generation, moderating prices of food grains and by streamlining marketing arrangements.

45

Food, Fun and Quality of Life

THE broad theme of poverty continues to be the fertile ground for economists to plough. Abhijit Banerjee's latest book '*Poor Economics: Rethinking Poverty and the Ways to End it*, written jointly with his Massachusetts Institute of Technology (MIT) Colleague Easter Dufla has created a storm internationally for the interesting insights it offers. In an interview to a Mumbai financial daily he said "The World's poor don't just want better nutrition—They want fun and excitement too" (*Economic Times*, November 25, 2011). Commenting on India's proposed National Food Security Bill, Banerjee admits that India is one of the worst performers in nutrition. "If you look at nutrition rates in India, they are worse than that of Sub-Saharan Africa, though India is much richer than Sub-Saharan Africa. However, it is not enough for experts to say that you are not eating enough."

Dr Banerjee raises the question if a poor man gets one more rupee, how much of that rupee goes into nutrition. At most 30 per cent. What does the person do with the rest of the rupee? The person spends it on fun things—on tastier food, rather than on nutritious food. He cites the case of a classic starving poor in Morocoọ. Even when he had not enough to eat, he had his TV, his antenna and his DVD player. When asked why do you have this television when there is not enough to eat? His answer was: Television is more important than food. You have to think of life where pleasure has its space. Beyond a point, the poor seem to prefer pleasure to food. Banerjee seems to hint that the idea of providing say 30 kgs of rice per person per month under the food security umbrella is misconceived.

Banerjee reiterates that the poor need to have some space to have some pleasure. "They are always looking for some cheap ways to improve the quality of their lives like the rest of us. You might think that they can add some calories. But they trade off calories for some amount of pleasure and excitement, something new. It is very human".

I would submit that this is an amateurish appreciation of the more complicated issues involved. Fun and pleasure are not the appropriate words in the context.

If we probe deeper we find that media hype may many times distort consumer preferences, both in developed and developing economies. For instance, in India younger men today may prefer to buy a bottle of coke at ₹ 12 in preference to a glass of milk at the same price. Milk is wholesome food. Or, another young man may choose to buy junk food like potato chips or wafers in preference to the traditional wholesome food like *idli sambar or jhunka bhakri*. These distortions in consumer preferences are created by advertisements or media and are far from rational. Such distortions may add to excitement and fun but it is facetious to argue that they contribute to improvement in the quality of life, as Banerjee seems to believe.

We should go back to the old philosophic proposition that man cannot live by bread alone. Let me illustrate this with the concrete case of India's development planning. India's First Five Year Plan (1951) opens with these words:

> The central objective of planning in India at the present stage is to initiate a process of development which will raise the living standards and open out to people new opportunities for richer and more varied life... But the economic condition of a country at any given time is a product of a broader social environment, and economic planning has to be viewed as an integral part of a wider process aiming not merely at the development in a narrow technical sense, but at the development of human faculties and the building up of an institutional framework adequate to the needs and aspirations of the people.

Viewed against this broader background, equating eating tastier food and watching television with improving the quality of life seems to be too simplistic an interpretation, which is clouded by American economic thinking. Quality of life has a much broader connotation as India's First Plan has enunciated.

The state has to play a proactive role in discouraging such distortions and more positively in opening out to people "new opportunities for richer and varied life". In this context it may be appropriate to refer to a book written by me jointly with Professor J.R. Bellerby of Oxford University, which provided what we called a Periphal Plan aimed at improving the quality of life (J.R. Bellerby and N.A. Mujumdar, 1960. *Agricultural Economic Theory and the Indian Economy*). Such periphal plan would supplement the technical or the engineering plan.

This peripheral plan dealt more directly with fundamental social aims of development schemes: literacy as part of social education; measures concerned with health, sports and culture. People in rural India have preserved the traditional culture which finds expression in music and dances and in festivals with displays and recitals of folk ballads in the form of cradle songs, marriage songs, harvest songs—in which every important happening in the life of an individual or a group is celebrated. Similarly, there is indigenous art manifesting itself in pottery, handicrafts and painting. Some aspects of the peripheral plan may be concerned with increase in wealth though indirectly like education. All action arising from this plan is for the average citizens. The state may provide guidelines, opportunity, finance and even leadership. But progress in this area is always indirect, *via* the innumerable voluntary organisations and beneficiaries. Implementation of such a plan would go a long way towards improving the quality of life.

Surely it is not the intention of anyone to force 32 kgs of rice down the throat of an unwilling consumer. The state merely tries to provide economic access to this quantity of food grains. If somebody wants to reject wholesome food in preference to junk food so be it. But it is the business of the state to educate such consumers about what is right for them because such distorted preferences are a result of lack of education and media hype. Quality of life is a much broader concept and the state has to address these broader concerns.

46

Hunger Insurance is of Prime Importance

IT may be recalled that the World Food Summit and the Millennium Summit had set the target of reducing world poverty and hunger by half from 1990 to 2015. According to World Bank (WB) data—these targets have been achieved by 2010—well in advance of the target year. Is there room for complacency?

Fresh thinking on poverty and undernourishment has made some analysts question this conclusion. According to the Food and Agriculture Organisation (FAO), hunger and calorific undernourishment have increased in absolute terms, over the last decade (*The State of Food Security in the World*, 2008). Basically, the WB's poverty line—money-metric of $125 a day at 2005 prices—is methodologically flawed and is hardly useful for policy purposes. For instance, from the policy point of view, it is the absolute number of hungry people that is really important and not so much proportions. Jorno Kwane Sundaram of FAO, in a recent thought-provoking essay on 'Poverty Matters', makes out a strong case for social provisioning for and protection of the hungry in developing countries including middle-income countries (MICs) like India. Further, he stresses that "a basic social protection floor" is affordable in most countries (*Economic & Political Weekly*, December 8, 2012). These issues need to be debated widely.

At the aggregate level, the decline in poverty level has been influenced by China, which recorded a sharp decline in its poverty. By virtue of their size, China and India taken together had accounted for 42 per cent of the chronically hungry people in the developing world. This has now changed. In the 1990s, 93 per cent of the world's poor lived in low-income countries (LICs). In 2007-08, 75 per cent of the poor lived in middle-income countries (MICs). Four countries India,

Pakistan, Indonesia and Nigeria account for the shift, as these have now graduated into MICs.

Turning to India, we do take pride in the fact that it has been possible to reduce the poverty levels over the years. This is clearly reflected in the poverty ratio figures. The Planning Commission figures indicate that poverty declined from 36 per cent of the population in 1993-94 to 27.5 per cent in 2004-05, a reduction of 8.5 percentage points. Even if one were to go by the Tendulkar Committee estimates, although the headcount ratios for both 1993-94 and 2004-05 are higher than the Planning Commission data, the extent of poverty reduction over the period is almost the same, at 8.1 percentage points. What is important to underline is this reduction has not prevented the extent of undernourishment from rising. According to FAO, the number of undernourished rose from 207 million in 1990-1992 to 231 million in 2003-2005. That is 24 million more undernourished persons were added during this period. This was a result of deceleration of food supply per capita, which was accompanied by higher food requirements per capita. From the policy point of view therefore it is not enough to take into account the headcount poverty ratios alone but also superimpose undernourishment data on them. The policy responses would have to be more nuanced to tackle the complex situation.

Apart from these supply-demand imbalances, there are what one might call 'external shocks' which impinge on the poor. The sharp rise in world food prices played havoc with the poor. For instance, the FAO Index of real food prices began rising in 2002, after four decades of primarily declining trends, and spiked sharply in 2006 and 2007. By mid-2008, real food prices were 64 per cent higher than their 2002 levels. FAO estimates that mainly as a result of high food prices, the number of chronically hungry people in the world rose by 75 million in 2007 to reach 923 million. The devastating effect of high food prices on the number of hungry people is thus clear. Similarly, the global financial crisis occurred close on the heels of the sharp rise in food prices. The UN estimates that between 47 million and 64 million additional people fell into and were thus trapped in extreme poverty because of the crisis (*UN Report on World Social Situation*, 2012).

Methodologically, critics point out the weak empirical basis for the country and global poverty numbers, used by the WB. Further, the inadequacy of measures based on food intake—calorific intake—for nutritional assessment has now been recognised. Long ago, Dr Sukhatme in his pioneering work on nutrition, explained that the conversion efficiency of food into energy of an individual depends on his access to safe drinking water, health care and environmental hygiene. In a broader perspective, the experience of poverty is now being viewed as multi-dimensional. Deprivation, social exclusion and lack of participation—all these form part of the poverty phenomenon. We are therefore moving towards the new Multi-dimensional Poverty Index (MPI), which covers some 10 indicators of social development.

All these have important implications for policy. Growth is necessary for poverty reduction and correction of nutritional deficiencies, but not enough. Growth should be job-rich. We need to adopt heterodox development policies to mitigate the negative impact of external shocks to prevent people from falling in deeper poverty. It is in this context that a basic social protection floor becomes necessary. International Labour Organization (ILO) estimates that only about 20 per cent of the world's working population has access to comprehensive social protection. Hence there is need to provide some sort of insurance against hunger.

At present we are trying to provide food security by an omnibus approach, namely the Food Security Act. There are apprehensions that the proposed arrangements are not workable. First, given the track record of the Food Corporation of India (FCI), procurement and distribution of food grains on such a mass scale implicit in the Food Security Act is not easy to implement. Second, subsidising the total quantum of food grains which is implicit in the Food Security Act is not fiscally feasible. As it is, the incidence of large subsidies on the budget is reflected in the deficits which are beyond comfort level. We therefore need to take a second look at our basic approach to food security. A more nuanced policy response is warranted. We should identify the most vulnerable sections of the population and offer protection to this section, if necessary by offering full subsidy for food grains supplied to them through the public distribution system (PDS). The food requirements of the rest of the population can be met through the normal market mechanism. This will not impose any additional burden on food administration. This offers a pragmatic solution to food security, a solution which is fiscally viable.

VI

Global Environment

47

Reflections on the American Financial Mess

NOW that the initial panic reaction to the downgrading of the US long-term debt, by the Standard and Poor's, from triple A to AA+, on Friday the 5th August, has mellowed down, it is time to reflect calmly on the more basic macroeconomic factors that led to the situation. The stock markets reaction was far from rational. The Dow Jones was down by 600 points or by 4.5 per cent and the conflaggeration spread enveloping both developed and emerging market economies: the UK, Germany, France and Japan, and Hongkong, South Korea and Taiwan. In India the Sensex dipped 316 point to touch 16,990. Irrational fear seems to have gripped the stock markets. The stock markets are said to be goaded by two factors, namely greed and fear, forget the fundamentals. This episode lends credence to the statement. The proof of pudding is in the eating. The auctions of Treasury Bills on Monday, the 8th August, attracted larger inflow of funds, driving the yield down. Who would want to invest funds in a sinking economy?

This panic reaction was totally unwarranted for the following four reasons:

First, the downgrading was by only one agency. The other two major rating agencies Moody and Fitch continued to rate the Federal Government bonds as triple A.

Second, this downgrading happened close on the heels of President Obama successfully negotiating an agreement on debt ceiling and budget cutting arrangements on 2nd August. This was an occasion for celebration and not downgrading.

Third, the US economy has recorded a deceleration in growth and not a recession. GDP growth was 1.6 per cent in the second quarter: though not flattering, this is not negative growth.

Finally, and more fundamentally, since when have we begun to take seriously the pronouncements of credit rating agencies? In the global financial crisis of 2008, when the icons of American and European financial system, commercial banks, investment banks, mortgage houses, and insurance giants collapsed like a pack of cards, what were these rating agencies doing? Even some junk derivatives had received triple A ratings from these worthies.

In the context of the totality of the world economy, there is another unique factor about the US economy we have to reckon with the TINA (there is no alternative) factor; there is no alternative. The US has been a super economic power and continues to remain so, with warts and all. Hence President Obama's pronouncement about the present American financial mess seems to be justified. "No matter what a credit rating agency says, America was and will always be an AAA country".

Let us go back to August 1971 when America decided unilaterally to float the US dollar. This shook the very foundations of International Monetary Fund (IMF) which was administering a fixed exchange regime, with US dollar linked to gold. With the US unilateral decision, the gold link was snapped and the sanctimonious fixed exchange rate regime received a death blow. IMF looked on helplessly and it had to learn to live in a world of floating currencies. The US has thus always called the tune for international financial system. The then, US Treasury Secretary Connaly's words still linger in our mind: "The U.S. dollar exchange rate is not for negotiation".

Why has the US dollar remained the only reserve currency today? Historically, there was pound sterling which was an important reserve currency with its own sterling area. It met its demise under the weight of reserve currency burden. Both Germany and Japan two candidates for reserve currency have discouraged Central Banks to invest in their bonds. Hence whether one likes or not, the US remains the only destination for Governments/Central Banks to invest. In fact part of the US debt is "involuntary debt" because the investment takes place not because the US wants it but because the investor has nowhere else to go. Even countries which are not necessarily friendly to the US have to perforce invest. For instance, China is the biggest foreign investor in the US Treasury bonds, with its holdings reaching $1.2 trillion.

Earlier, IMF's quixotic efforts to promote a paper currency the Special Drawing Rights (SDR) also proved abortive. Initially hopes were pinned on the euro which was expected to emerge as a reserve currency but alas! these hopes foundered because of the debt problems of Portugal, Greece, Italy and Spain.

Some experts like Dr S.S. Tarapore advocate that Central Banks should invest a sizeable proportion of their reserves in gold. Some countries like France are already doing it. But in this case what is good for one country or Central Bank may not necessarily be good for the system as a whole. For the system, it would be tantamount to sterilising financial resources which are productive into a dead asset, namely gold.

What are the immediate policy implications of the American financial mess for India? Both the Finance Minister and Reserve Bank of India (RBI) have responded to this question. The Finance Minister has reassured that India's growth story is intact the growth forecasts vary from 8.2 per cent to 8.5 per cent. In fact the softening of international commodity prices, especially of oil, would help check inflation pressures in the domestic economy and maintain fiscal balance in 2011-12. Government would stick to its target of capping the fiscal deficit to 4.6 per cent of GDP in 2011-12.

India continues to be an attractive investment destination to foreign institutional investors (FIIs), in view of the higher returns that global investors could get in India. Foreign direct investment (FDI) in India rose over four times in June 2011 to reach $5.15 billion as compared to $1.38 billion a year ago.

RBI, on its part, has indicated its readiness to intervene in the markets to avoid any volatility in domestic markets. "In the immediate future, the Reserve Bank's priority is to ensure that adequate rupee and forex liquidity are maintained in domestic markets to prevent excessive volatility in interest rates and exchange rates". There is no strain on liquid reserves to meet the demand for forex even in stress scenarios.

Monetary policy will have to perhaps face the toughest challenge. The stubbornly high inflation is hovering around 9 per cent. In fact food inflation soared to 9.9 per cent in the week ending July 30, 2011. This re-emphasises the need to further monetary tightening. In sharp contrast, in order to revive the economy the Federal Reserve System in the US would embark on a third round of Quantitative Easing (QE3). It has already indicated that the present low interest rates would continue. There is a lobby in India which advocates that we should ape this policy by reversing monetary fiscal tightening, as we did in the 2008 crisis. This would be a grave error and our over-riding priority should continue to be expeditiously crushing the high inflation.

48

Global Slowdown and Financial Stability

THE continued global slowdown and the deepening crisis in the Euro area cloud the external environment today. There are signs of spillover of the developments in the Eurozone to the emerging and developing economies (EDEs). Against this background the *Financial Stability Report* (FSR) issued by the Reserve Bank of India (RBI) in June 2012 assumes special significance. Through these half-yearly FSRs, RBI seeks to share the results of macro prudential surveillance with the market, identify the vulnerable segments and initiate prompt corrective actions, wherever needed. This is the fifth report in the series.

The report sums up the situation as follows: threats to stability of the financial system are posed by, externally, the sovereign default concerns in the Eurozone which have escalated fears of contagion and recession. Domestically, worsening fiscal position, widening current account deficit and structural aspects of food inflation are causes of worry. Although falling international crude oil prices are a silver lining, below normal monsoon has added to the anxieties. The report had assumed normal monsoon. On the banking system, the report is up-beat: "Indian banks' soundness indicators remained robust, although the pressures on asset quality persisted".

For instance, the contagion effect manifested itself on July 23, when stocks crashed in Asia, on worries that Spain may have to opt for a sovereign bailout package. Our own Sensex declined by 281 points to touch 16,877. The report provides some useful insights into the domestic factors that pose a threat to stability, as mentioned above. The widening current account deficit is due in part to gold imports which have been sustained at a high level. India imported $45 billion worth of gold in 2011-12—3 per cent more over the previous year.

Gold imports constitute as much as 10 per cent of total imports. I have all along argued that permitting unbridled gold imports in the name of liberalisation was a policy blunder. A poor country can't afford to lock up large resources in an unproductive asset like gold when the investment needs are enormous. According to a World Gold Council study, only about 23 per cent of total gold imports may be for 'investment' and the rest for jewellery. The so-called investment is in a dead asset. At last the RBI admits "Diversion of household savings into gold has implications for the availability of funds for the financial sector and thereby for growth". It is high time the Government takes some drastic measures to moderate gold imports.

The 2012-13 Union Budget sets out a road map for fiscal consolidation by budgeting a significant reduction in the ratio of gross fiscal deficit to GDP, beginning from 2012-13. However, economic developments in the current fiscal year have turned out to be quite disturbing. Sharp deceleration in GDP and persisting inflation, have brought about a slippage in the deficit target, envisaged in the budget. The actual deficit may turn out to be around 5.6 per cent of GDP. Increased market borrowings by Government could crowd out private investment with implications for growth. Will the Government be able to contain its expenditure on subsidies within the stipulated cap of 2 per cent of GDP in 2012-13? The fiscal risks are daunting, especially when the semi-drought conditions are staring at us in the current fiscal year. Risk perceptions have thus worsened since the publication of FSR.

The banking scenario looks quite comfortable. The present regulatory requirements stipulate that banks in India maintain a capital ratio of 9 per cent of risk weighted assets (RWAs), which is higher than the 8 per cent prescribed by the Basel Committee. Credit growth in the banking sector decelerated to 16.3 per cent in 2011-12 from the level of 22.6 per cent in the previous year. This reflects the overall slowdown in GDP growth. Deposit growth decelerated sharply to some 14 per cent—the lowest growth rate recorded in the past 10 years. This led to increased reliance of banks on borrowed funds. Liquidity risks have perhaps increased. The gross non-performing assets (NPA) rose to 2.9 per cent of total assets as at the end of March

2012, from the level of 2.4 per cent at the end of March 2011. But the report adds: "The position is not alarming at the current juncture and some comfort is also provided by the strong capital adequacy of banks". On the whole, the report is reassuring on the banking system. Nonetheless, the asset quality concerns of banks persist and the report calls for a closer look at the underlying management of NPAs by bank.

Another cause of concern which the report underlines is the rapid rise of gold companies. The exponential growth in the balance sheets of Non-banking Financial Companies (NBFCs) engaged in lending against gold in recent years poses some risks to bank, for two reasons. First, these companies depend highly on borrowing from banks. Second, the rapid rise in gold prices. This growing interconnectedness of gold loan companies with banks has sought to be addressed by RBI through some regulatory measures.

Inflation continue to haunt the economy. Wholesale price index (WPI) which was above 9 per cent in April-November 2011 moderated to 6.9 per cent by the end of March 2012. However WPI rose to 7 per cent in May 2012, driven by mainly food and fuel prices. More worrying, the consumer price index (CPI) has risen sharply to double digit figure in April 2012. Thus the FSR is a useful document for a number of reasons. It brings some transparency in the developments in the financial system, promotes informed debate and hopefully leads to some soul searching by concerned financial entities so that corrective action could be taken wherever needed.

49

Crash of Capitalism

Need to Revive Ethical Values

A series of corruption scandals are clouding the socioeconomic scene today. Social scientists, however, must recognise that corruption is a symptom of a far more deep and widespread malaise that afflicts the society and must seek to address the basic malaise. For instance, corruption is not confined to political circles only. In sports, cricket is notorious for corruption episodes. Recently, a film star has produced a documentary illustrating with concrete cases how low medical ethics has sunk. Similarly, in the academic field, there are episodes of marks manipulation, mass copying, and nepotism in the appointment of Vice Chancellors, and so on.

Since 1991, we have been following the American capitalist model for macro-management of the economy. Corporate America's fall from grace has been sudden and complete. Investigations of the 2008 financial meltdown have laid bare the shameless greed and moral degradation of the Wall Street bankers. All these have led to a call, for reviving ethical and moral values not only among corporates and bankers but also among all sections of the population. Economics has been defined sometimes as a study of man in the ordinary business of life. Have we been focusing exclusively 'on the ordinary business of life' and ignored the 'man'?

Let us begin with the collapse of the American capitalist model.

Recent revelations of corporate crookedness and accounting scandals in America have shaken the very foundations of the American capitalist model. Corporate America's fall from the grace has been sudden and complete. The Enron, Worldcom and Xerox exposures have unveiled the darker side of western style capitalism where, in the quest for short-term gains, wrongdoings are overlooked. The collapse of Andersen, one of the big five accounting firms has, in the wake of Enron scandal, added a new dimension to the systemic infirmities.

This 'corporate-accounting firm-capital market' nexus perhaps proved to be the last straw on the back of the American capitalist system. Fudging of accounts seems to have evolved into a fine art. The depth of degradation to which unbridled corporate greed can lead has become all too obvious. These developments cannot be dismissed, as some apologists of American capitalism are doing, as isolated incidents. They are systemic. According to Prof Lester C. Thurow of the Solan School of Management at Massachusetts Institute of Technology (MIT): "The Enrons and Worldcoms are not abnormalities in a basically sound system. Scandals are endemic to capitalism". *The Economist*, London, summed up the situation: "Chief Executives and accountants have became a dispised breed less trusted than politicians and journalists". All these happenings took place around 2002.

Move over to the global financial crisis of 2008, which reflected in all its rawness, the workings of predatory financial capitalism. When the icons of American and European financial system commercial banks, investment banks, mortgage houses and insurance giants collapsed like a pack of cards, what happened to the mythology built around the private financial institutions like capital adequacy norms, Basle norms, provisioning requirements, asset-liability management, risk-weighted lending rates and credit-rating systems. Why did not this paraphernalia of devices emit warning signals that the whole edifice is about to crumble? It was not so much the institutional infirmities as the corporate greed and the culture that nourishes such greed that was responsible for the catastrophy. The financial crisis in the US started as a sub-prime mortgage crisis. A fast growing new breed of lenders were luring many people into risky mortgages they could not afford. With incentives for aggressive loan disbursements, banks poured billions of dollars into poor households often with incomplete documents. The unquestioned faith in the status of triple A credit rating led to buying of billions of structured bonds which later turned out to be worth nothing, since the market for a number of structured products became non-existent during the period of financial meltdown. Thus it was not merely mortgage houses, but also investment banks, accountants and credit raters who were involved in the drama. The Financial

Crisis Inquiry Commission has laid bare for all to see the shameless greed and moral decadence of Wall Street banker. The 'Occupy Wall Street' movement reflects the public resentment over the behaviour of financial actors.

More recently, by fixation of London Inter-bank Offered Rate (LIBOR) and credit rating, the major global players in the financial markets discredited themselves their unfair practices stand exposed. In a similar vein there is the case of management icon Rajat Gupta who sold his soul for a mess of pottage. The central theme is therefore that corporate greed, crookedness and self-centredness and a culture that nourishes these qualities all these are symptomatic of a sickness that afflicts society—a sickness born of moral pollution.

In response to these unsavoury developments, there is a call for revival of ethical values. The American Economic Association has mooted the idea of code of ethics for finance professionals, regulators and academics. More explicitly, Robert Shiller in his recent book *Finance and the Good Society* (2012) proposes that "the best way to do this is to build good moral behavior into the culture of Wall Street through the creation and observance of best practices in its various professions—CEOs, traders, accountants, investment bankers, lawyers philanthropists". What is our response? If improvement in the quality of life is the end-objective of all development endeavours, the need to tackle such sickness becomes imperative.

Indian philosophy offers a remedy. It advocates the need to build 'development conscience' among all sections of the population. From times immemorial Indian philosophy has maintained that the all-round development of a society is best achieved through the betterment of the individual, which no doubt includes economic well-being but extends well beyond it. Social conscience must be inculcated among individuals through education at all stages and also professional training. All individuals must be sensitised at their young age itself to the abject poverty, the squalor, disease, ignorance and illiteracy that surround us. They must be made to begin to think in terms of what is their *dharma* or duty towards alleviating some of the infirmities that afflict our less fortunate fellow human beings.

The *Bhagavad Gita* enjoins us to treat others as you treat yourself. What is good for you is good for others; what is bad for you is bad for others. Learn to rejoice in doing good to all creatures.

One of the ancient scriptures of India the *Brahadarnyaka Upanishad* enjoins that our life must be guided by the following three *Das*, *Damyata*, that is control yourself, *Datta*, that is give to others, and Dayadhvam, that is be compassionate. Thus we must practise self-control, charity and compassion. Inculcating these qualities among individuals would go a long way towards eliminating corruption, improving the quality of life, and in general evolving a compassionate society.

50

Capitalism and the Compassionate Society

THE *Economic Survey 2010-11*, issued by Government of India in February 2011, has added a new dimension to economic development, as it were, and this aspect which has not attracted much attention needs to be discussed widely because of its broader policy implications. In a small sub-section entitled "Social Basis of Economic Progress", the Survey declares: "What is increasingly recognised is that successful economic development has a strong correlation with these human qualities of honesty and trustworthiness. The drive for greater profit and greater personal utility, devoid of these social qualities, creates a dysfunctional and chaotic society" (p.48).

Again, "So once we recognise that honesty, integrity, and trustworthiness are not just good moral qualities in themselves but qualities, which, when imbibed by a society, lead to economic progress and human development, people will have a tendency to acquire these qualities, and that should help build a more tolerant and progressive society" (p.41).

While this approach to development makes a good beginning, it should be pointed out that it reflects a narrow understanding of the phenomenon which forms part of the larger systemic infirmities causing moral pollution. I have discussed these broader philosophical issues in the article "The Development Conscience Factor" included in the book: *Economic Reforms Sans Development* published in 2004. Let me recapitulate the main points. Recent revelations of corporate crookedness and accounting scandals in America have shaken the very foundations of the American capitalist model. Corporate America's fall from grace has been sudden and complete.

The Enron, Worldcom and Xerox exposures have unveiled the darker side of western style capitalism where, in the quest for short-term gains, wrongdoings are overlooked. The collapse of Andersen, one of the big five accounting firms has, in the wake of Enron scandal, added a new dimension to the systemic infirmities. This "corporate-accounting firm-capital market" nexus perhaps proved to be the last straw on the back of the American capitalist system. Fudging of accounts seems to have evolved into a fine art. The depth of degradation to which unbridled corporate greed can lead has become all too obvious. These developments cannot be dismissed, as some apologists of American capitalism are doing, as isolated incidents. They are systemic. According to Professor Lester C. Thurow of the Solan School of Management at Massachusetts Institution of Technology (MIT): "The Enrons and Worldcoms are not abnormalities in a basically sound system. Scandals are endemic to capitalism". *The Economist*, London, summed up the situation: "Chief Executives and accountants have become a dispised breed less trusted than politicians and journalists". All these happenings took place around 2002.

Move over to the global financial crisis of 2008, which reflected in all its rawness, the workings of predatory financial capitalism. When the icons of American and European financial system commercial banks, investment banks, mortgage houses and insurance giants collapsed like a pack of cards, what happened to the mythology built around the private financial institutions like capital adequacy norms, Basel norms, provisioning requirements, asset-liability management, risk-weighted lending rates and credit-rating systems. Why did not this paraphernalia of devices emit warning signals that the whole edifice is about to crumble? It was not so much the institutional infirmities as the corporate greed and the culture that nourishes such greed that was responsible for the catastrophy. The financial crisis in the US started as a sub-prime mortgage crisis. A fast growing new breed of lenders were luring many people into risky mortgages they could not afford. With incentives for aggressive loan disbursements, banks poured billions of dollars into poor households often with incomplete documents. The unquestioned faith in the status of triple A credit rating led to buying of billions of structured bonds which later turned out to be worth nothing, since the market for a number of structured products became non-existent during the period of financial meltdown. Thus it was not merely mortgage houses, but also investment banks, accountants and credit raters who were involved in the drama. The Financial Crisis Inquiry Commission has laid bare for all to see the shameless greed and moral decadence of Wall Street banker.

The central issue therefore is that corporate greed, crookedness and self-centredness and a culture that nourishes these qualities all these are symptomatic of a sickness that afflicts society—a sickness born of moral pollution. Such sickness frustrates economic growth and development in emerging market economies like India, or erode the quality of life in the case of advanced economies like be the US.

If improvement in the quality of life is the end-objective of all development endeavours, the need to tackle such sickness becomes imperative. Indian philosophy offers a remedy. It advocates the need to build 'development conscience' among all sections of the population. From times immemorial Indian philosophy has maintained that the all-round development of a society is best achieved through the betterment of the individual, which no doubt includes economic well-being but extends well beyond it. Social conscience must be inculcated among individuals through education at all stages and also professional training. All individuals must be sensitised at their young age itself to the abject poverty, the squalor, disease, ignorance and illiteracy that surround us. They must be made to begin to think in terms of what is their *dharma* or duty towards alleviating some of the infirmities that afflict our less fortunate fellow human beings.

One of the ancient scriptures of India, the *Brahadarnyaka Upanishad* enjoins that our life must be guided by the following three *Das*: *Damyata*, that is control yourself, *Datta*, that is give to others, and Dayadhvam, that is be compassionate. Thus we must practise self-control, charity and compassion. Inculcating these qualities among individuals would go a long way towards improving the quality of life and in general evolving a compassionate society.

51

Under-belly of Predatory Financial System

RECENTLY, the Prime Minister exhorted the mandarins of the Finance Ministry to revive the animal spirits of the Indian industrialists with a view to giving a boost to the growth of the economy which has slowed down. When we talk of animal spirits in this context, what we have in mind is the image of the Schumpeterian hero—who gathers the factors of production, land, labour and capital, innovates, faces the competition of the market and makes a success of his firm. If there is no market, he creates the market for his product. That is the beauty of capitalism. But there is an ugly face of capitalism which reflects the beastly spirits of entrepreneurs and this face is assuming larger proportions in more recent years, especially in the financial sector. This aspect has not attracted adequate attention in economic literature.

Let us begin with "The US economic crisis of historic proportions" to use the words of President Obama, of 2008. The crisis was triggered by the financial meltdown when the icons of American and European system—commercial banks, investment banks, mortgage houses, and insurance giants—collapsed like a pack of cards. If the world economic crisis of the 1930s was called the 'Great Depression' it would not be an exaggeration to call the 2008 crisis as a 'Great Fraud', because the fraud was systemic and not confined to any institution or a segment of the financial system. The financial crisis started as a subprime mortgage crisis in August 2007. In simple terms, housing loans were extended aggressively to borrowers who did not have the capacity to repay. The traditional banking prudence was thrown to the wind. It was reckless lending. Many subprime mortgages were 'ninja loans', standing for no income, no job and no assets. Super imposed on this subprime lending was the securitisation of debt process. This process is described as "a package of dodgy debts of some Alabama Unemployed Man turned into a High Grade Structured Enhanced Leverage Fund of a leading Wall Street Firm". When the crunch occurred, these sophisticated structured credit products proved to be not worth the paper they were printed on.

Parenthetically, we should add that Dr Reddy, the then RBI Governor, successfully resisted the pressures to introduce such credit products in India. He was dubbed as a 'Conservative'. In this global financial crisis, the Indian financial system dominated by the public sector and untainted by financial 'innovative' products stood rock-like.

Our contemporary policy-makers do not seem to have learnt any lessons from this recent episode. Their admiration of the private financial system remains undiluted. They listen respectfully to Raghuram Rajan who states: "The majority of this committee does not see a compelling reason for continuing government ownership" of financial institutions (2008-09). In fact we should advise Raghuram Rajan that the rationale for privatisation, if any, has now evapourated. We see no reason why we should privatise reverting to the main theme. Joseph Stigliz, the Nobel Laureate, writes about how bankers mulcted their institutions: "It would be one thing if the high incomes of those at the top were the result of greater contributions to society but the Great Recession (global economic crisis of 2008) showed otherwise: bankers who had led the global economy to the brink of ruin received outsize bonuses" (*Economic Times*, June 11, 2012). Even when bailout by the US, to revive the institutions, the CEOs helped themselves generously with obscenely high bonuses. Thus it was the unbridled greed of bankers of the private financial sector which was at the root of the 2008 crisis.

Simon Johson, the former Chief Economist of the International Monetary Fund (IMF), recently came out with more disturbing revelations. The bankers' activities reflect the face of predatory financial capitalism. Some of these 'risks' resembled pure gambling activities. When the going is good, bankers benefit. When things go wrong they seek shelter under government-run subsidy schemes, the kind of bailout packages we witnessed in the 2008 crisis. What is more, to protect the continuation of such subsidy schemes global mega-banks contribute large amount of money to politicians. For instance, it is estimated that J.P. Morgan Chase, the US largest bank holding company, spent around $8 million in political contributions in 2011. It is shocking to see how 'too-big-to-fail' bankers sustain their implicit subsidies.

That is not all. In support of their political strategy global mega banks also run a highly sophisticated disinformation/propaganda mission. They create a veneer of responsibility for the subsidies that they receive by roping in academicians from prestigious universities. Simon cites concrete cases of involvement of academicians from Stanford and Columbia universities. Some of these prominent academicians received large sums to support the interests of large banks—their excessive risk-taking sharp practices, innovative financial products and so on. Academic support for predatory financial institutions was thus available, at a price. This is what Simon calls the "Unholy Nexus of Predators and Professors" (see Simons article in *Economic Times*, July 2, 2012).

Finally, the recent indictment of Rajat Gupta for insider trading has shocked the financial community. Even the jury convicting him felt sorry for him. He was an icon—the first non-American MD of Mckinsey and one of the founding fathers of the Indian School of Business, Hyderabad. Gupta had achieved remarkable success and acquired a stature for financial probity. Financially also, he was quite comfortable: his family networth is estimated at $130 million. Why did he sell his soul for a mess of pottage? The answer is: Greed, the beastly spirit of predatory capitalism.

Some of India's contemporary policy-makers are still haunted by the ghosts of market theology. It is necessary to persuade them to disengage themselves from the trappings of the outdated market theology and refrain them from mimicking the American models. The exposure of the under-belly of predatory financial capitalism should serve as refresher course material for them. They need not listen respectfully to the likes of Raghuram Rajan. We have our own institutions to serve the rural requirements: regional rural banks (RRBs) and cooperatives. The post office which has its feet deep in the rural sector has a great potential for emerging as a rural bank. We should revitalise these grass-roots institutions, rather than trying to establish new small private sector banks.

52

The Great Divide

The Royalty and the Publican

THE humble toilet has entered into the lofty discourse on development. Recently, the Planning Commission renovated its toilet at a cost of ₹ 37 lakhs triggering a debate on: Is this lavish expenditure justified? In fact to argue that since many foreigners visit the Planning Commission and therefore it needs a modern toilet is a weak defence because it reflects the inherited mode of colonial thinking. The Planning Commission and its staff deserve to have a decent toilet and nobody should grudge the expenditure. In fact this issue raises a much wider question of the great divide of the modern Indian society, say the post-reform phase since 1991—into the royalty and the publican.

Unfortunately for the Plan panel, the issue has arisen at a time when we are launching the sanitation drive, rechristened Nirmal Bharat Abhiyan aiming to promote use of toilets in the countryside to cut down open defecation that is linked to lack of hygiene leading to several diseases. It is estimated about 65 per cent of Indians defecate in the open. The Centre has increased the grant for toilets under the total sanitation campaign, from ₹ 4,600 to ₹ 10,000 per toilet. The campaign's target is 10 years for making the country free from open defecation.

It is legitimate to raise the question: Why did it take 60 years for the Planning Commission to tackle the issue of open defecation? Why did it not address this issue promptly as it did in renovating its own toilet facilities? The great divide between royalty and the publican!

In terms of public health, investment in sanitation is justified purely on economic ground: bad sanitation leads to diseases affecting the health and productivity of the people. Prevention is better than cure. This is besides improving the quality of life of the people, culturally and socially.

More basically, we live in the land of Mahatma Gandhi. We know his two obsessions: No Indian should starve and all Indians should live in clean environment. His frequent stays in *harijan* colonies were marked by himself taking a broom and cleaning the colony and establishing a rudimentary system of toilets. Much before development economists started talking about investment in human capital, the Mahatma had shown us the way. His picture with a broom in his hand has become part of the Gandhi folklore. The Plan panel does not seem to have been beneficiary of the Mahatma legacy.

Take another recent example. When former minister Shashi Tharoor was advised to move into a guest house from a five-star hotel, he was not amused. He was also asked to travel by economy class instead of the business class. He dubbed the economy class travel by air as 'Cattle Class.' It is not a question of whether the Centre's budgetary resources are adequate to finance stay in a five-star hotel or travel by business class. The point is that those engaged in public service—one assumes that Union Ministers are—in a poor country should set an example of modest living. The 'Cattle Class' remark reflects the divide between the royalty and the publican.

Gandhiji's another obsession was elimination of hunger. As long as even one person is starved, is malnourished or lacks decent housing, the social order stands indicated lacking legitimacy. It is common knowledge now that 40 per cent of our children are underfed and undernourished. Recently the Prime Minister called this phenomenon a matter of national shame. A part from other food management issues, the basic question of how we take care of our foodgrains stocks is revolting. The Food Corporation of India (FCI) allows the grains stocked in the open to rot in the rain or to be eaten by rats. Even recently TV channels have concretely shown how this is actually happening. But the Food Minister is complacent. In a recent interview to a financial paper he said: "We have modernised FCI godowns through computerisation. Sitting in my office, I know the quantity, quality and distribution of grain from each godown. We have put CCTV cameras to watch operations". Are the TV channels manipulating images of foodgrains rotting or being eaten away by rats? It is again one more instance of the royalty and publican divide.

India is the abode of the largest number of underfed and undernourished persons in the world and to allow callously foodgrains to be destroyed is nothing short of blasphemy.

Such divide may be more subtle. Take the National Rural Employment Guarantee Act (NREGA) which now employs about 5 crore rural households and which has emerged as the flagship poverty-alleviation programme. Evaluations by even outside agencies have applauded the scheme. There is a renewed emphasis on drought-proofing: 10 out of 21 new works permitted under NREGA relate to watershed development. About 50 per cent of employment under the scheme is claimed by women. The minimum wages for rural labour have become meaningful with the scheme. But the large and medium farmers' lobby is up against the scheme because it has raised rural wages. Some critics have gone to the extent of arguing that farming is becoming unviable because of higher wages.

This discourse takes us well beyond the textbook prescriptions on economic development. Indian philosophy has maintained that the all-round development of a society is best achieved through betterment of individuals. Social conscience must be inculcated among individuals through education. All individuals must be sensitised to abject poverty, the squalor, disease, ignorance and illiteracy that surround us. They must begin to think in terms of what is our *dharma* or duty towards alleviating some of the infirmities that affect, our less fortunate brotheren. Our ancient scriptures have enjoined us to practise self-control, charity and compassion. Collectively, these three characteristics constitute 'Development Conscience.' Building up such conscience among all sections of the population would go a long way towards bridging the great divide between the royalty and the publican and towards evolving a compassionate society—an ideal the Mahatma sought to achieve.

53

Social Costs of the Global Economic Crisis

THE financial and economic crisis suffered by the world in 2008-09 was worst than the Great Depression of the 1930s. The global financial crisis occurred close on the heels of a sharp rise in global food and energy prices in 2007 and 2008 and hence had a devastating impact on the poor. The number of people living in hunger in the world soared to over a billion in 2009, the highest on record. It is estimated that between 47 million and 84 million additional people fell into and were trapped in extreme poverty because of the crisis. The UN *Report on the World Social Situation* (2012) explores the ongoing adverse social consequences of the crisis. The global economic downturn has had wider-ranging negative social consequences for individual communities and societies and its impact on social progress in areas such as education and health will only become fully manifest overtime. The report sounds a note of warning: "Given the fragility of the economic recovery and the uneven progress in major economies, social conditions are expected to recover only slowly. The increased levels of poverty, hunger and unemployment will continue to affect billions of people for years to come."

It is understandable why the severity of the crisis has not received adequate appreciation in India. First, the Indian financial system dominated by the public sector and untainted by the so-called structured credit products remained stable, unaffected by the crisis. Second, in terms of GDP growth there was a slowdown but not a sharp decline. The annual global growth rate declined from about 4 per cent during 2006-07 to 1.6 per cent in 2008, and further to -2 per cent in 2009. Ninety-five countries experienced declines in average per capita income.

In contrast, the deceleration in GDP growth in India was moderate from 8.4 per cent in 2010-11 to 6.5 per cent in 2011-12.

The financial crisis originated in developed countries no doubt, but its impact was transmitted to developing countries through international trades, commodity prices and higher costs of borrowing. This was especially true of those developing countries which were integrated into international markets. In India we are now witnessing its lagged effects. For instance, India's export growth which had lost momentum in the second half of 2011-12, mainly owing to slowdown in external demand, has shown further deterioration in 2012-13. Exports in April-September 2012-13 declined by 6.8 per cent as compared to the level during the corresponding period of 2011-12. There was considerable decline in exports to the Euro area. A more demonstrable case of external sector affecting India's growth is the risks from the impending US 'Fiscal Cliff'. As the RBI puts it: "A major downside risk to global growth is now looming from the US fiscal cliff. The US Congressional Budget office forecasts that the US fiscal deficit will decline by 3.3 percentage points to 4 per cent of GDP in 2013. Such as sharp fiscal consolidation may have a deleterious impact on global growth. There could be an adverse impact of the US fiscal cliff on India's growth. If global growth slumps, there would be spilled over impact on the current account as well...." It now seems difficult for India to attain even a 5 per cent GDP growth in 2012-13. Thus the full impact of the global financial and economic crisis on the Indian economy is now manifesting itself.

In retrospect a puzzling aspect of the crisis which emerges is: many international organisations were not preparing themselves to face the calamity. Far from it, the crisis came as a surprise for them. The UN Report specifically mentions two conspicuous cases. First, the International Monetary Fund (IMF) which monitors global macrofinancial developments, maintained an optimistic view, and took sometime to realise that the crisis would soon engulf the whole world. "A month before the first tremors of the subprime mortgage crisis in the United States of America were felt, the IMF noted? The strong global expansion is continuing and projections for global growth in both 2007 and 2008 have been revised upwards...."

The other example is the Organisation for Economic Cooperation and Development (OECD). For instance, three months before the subprime market collapse in August 2007, the OECD took the view that: "the US slowdown was not heralding a period of worldwide economic weakness, unlike for instance in 2001. Rather a "smooth" balancing was to be expected with Europe taking over the baton from the US in driving OECD growth. Our central forecast remains indeed quite benign: a soft landing in the US, a strong and sustained recovery in Europe, a solid trajectory in Japan and buoyant activity in China and India." Something is basically wrong in our forecasting tools or techniques and in our ability to interpret economic developments. What are we doing to rectify the shortcomings?

Reverting to social costs of the crisis, the longer term adverse employment consequences are already visible and in many countries youth unemployment has reached alarming levels. Unemployment and underemployment are very high among young people of 15 to 24 years: at the end of 2009 there were 79 million unemployed young people and globally the rate of youth unemployment stood at 13 per cent. The September 2010 High-level Plenary Meeting of the 65th session of the General Assembly on the Millennium Development Goals called attention to the critical importance of productive employment and decent work as a means to achieve the goals. Promoting a job-rich recovery will lay the foundation for realising the goal of sustained, inclusive and equitable economic growth.

The devastating impact of the crisis on such a large number of people under-scores the importance of social protection for reducing the vulnerability of the poor. In fact social protection should not be viewed as a temporary measure to cushion the impact of the crisis but rather as an ongoing investment to promote sustained, inclusive and equitable economic growth.

The report has an important message for those developing countries like India which do not have universal formal social protection schemes. The disconnect between economic policies and their social consequences can create a vicious circle of slow growth and poor social progress. In India we need to take a fresh look at the present clamour for doing away with food subsidies or the critics of the National Rural Employment Guarantee Act (NREGA). Both of these measures serve an important social purpose.

54

Global Financial Crisis

Some Lessons for Central Banks

Introduction

The global financial crisis of 2008 has changed the policy-making landscape for Central Banks. Three aspects of these changes can be briefly discussed. First, some broad lessons for Central Banks from the experience of handling the crisis can be derived. These are summed up in Section II. Second, the crisis has resulted, in the advanced countries, in the erosion of trust and confidence of the society in the financial sector. These issues are taken up for discussion in Section III. The erosion is partly the result of a comprehensive regulatory capture. As Dr Reddy[1] puts it: "There is, perhaps, what may be described as unionisation of global capital against attempts by public policies to regulate the financial sector effectively". There is public resentment at several irregularities in the functioning of financial institutions and at obscenely high level of remuneration paid to senior management in some cases. How can this confidence be restored? Is inclusive finance the answer? Third, looking back at history, India offers a refreshing contrast. This is an occasion when we should pay tributes to the vision of the founding fathers of the Reserve Bank of India (RBI) and the policy-makers of the 1970s. Much before financial inclusion became internationally fashionable, the Indian policy-makers laid the foundation for financial inclusion. These issues are discussed in Section IV.

Lessons for Central Banks

It is now five years since the outbreak of global financial crisis in 2008. These years have been defining moments in the history of

---

1. Reddy (2012).

Central Banking. The developments during the period have challenged the intellectual framework and conventionally held beliefs about the functioning of the financial system and theory and practice of Central Banking. Financial stability has come to occupy the centre stage of policy-making.[2]

The crisis has triggered a wide-ranging debate on the role and responsibilities of Central Banks. What should be the right framework for monetary policy? Do we need to re-define the mandate of Central Banks independence? Although no definitive conclusions have emerged from the debate and hard thinking by Central Banking and academicians, the debate has continued and some broad lessons from the experience of handling the crisis can be derived. Let us enumerate some of them.

First, inflation targeting. Before the crisis, there was a broad intellectual consensus in favour of inflation targeting, that is, basing monetary policy on achieving a target inflation rate, usually as expressed in consumer prices. There are formal inflation targeting Central Banks like those in Canada, New Zealand and Thailand. This solely inflation targeting appeared to have worked well for some extended period, when price stability was accompanied by stable growth and low unemployment. Thus inflation targeting became 'fashionable' and even some experts in India began to advocate its adoption. The mainstream view before the crisis was that price stability and financial stability reinforce each other. The crisis has demonstrated that this is wrong. Price stability does not necessarily ensure financial stability. The crisis has proved that price inflation targeting alone is inadvisable and that the mandate of Central Banks should extend beyond price stability to include bank regulation and supervision, financial stability and preventing asset price bubbles. Reserve Bank of India's (RBI) multiple objectives approach with low inflation not necessarily a dominant, far less the sole objective, stands vindicated. Growth, employment and equity are among the other objectives.

2. Sharma (2012).

Second, bank regulation and supervision. There is a variety of regulatory models. In some countries, Central Bank is a purely monetary authority, with bank regulation and supervision entrusted to another agency. The global crisis was caused, in large part, by a lack of coordination and communication between Central Banks and supervisors. The consensus that seems to be emerging after the crisis is that in the interest of financial stability, it is optimal to entrust regulation and supervision of banks to Central Banks.

The third point relates to the role of Central Banks in preventing asset price bubbles. We have seen how price bubbles in housing can have destructive effects on the financial system or the economy as a whole. It has been now been conceded that preventing an asset price bubble should form part of the responsibility of a Central Bank. Whether this objective should be sought to be achieved through monetary action, proper or regulatory action should better be left to the concerned Central Bank to decide.

Fourth, should financial stability be explicitly included in the mandate of Central Banks? There is an ongoing debate on the issue. Of course, one could argue that financial stability is necessary but not a sufficient condition for achieving the conventional objectives of Central Banks like growth, employment and equity, to which we have referred earlier. Basically, defining stability in a precise, comprehensive and measurable manner is difficult. In any case, the involvement of Central Banks in the stability exercise is now accepted. It may be recalled that during the global crisis, Central Banks injected large doses of liquidity, as part of their lender-of-last-resort function to unfreeze the system. The need for fundamental changes in the way banks and financial institutions are regulated is recognised. At the international level, important steps have been taken under the auspices of G-20, Financial Stability Board (FSB) and Basel Committee on Banking Supervision (BCBS). The emerging framework includes ring-fencing of banking institutions with more and better quality capital under Basel III, appropriate framework for systemically important financial institutions (SIFIs), aligning compensation practices to prudent risk-taking. The RBI has now begun to conduct macro-prudential surveillance of the financial system, on an ongoing basis. The assessment of financial stability and their findings are shared with financial institutions, market players and the general public in the form of *Financial Stability Reports* (FSRs). The first report was published in March 2010 and the fifth in 2012.

Finally, autonomy of Central Banks. Central Bank independence is under assault following the global financial crisis of 2008. During the crisis, Government and Central Banks coordinated their efforts to launch unprecedented expansionary fiscal and monetary policies. As countries now contemplate exiting these extraordinary expansion policies, the familiar conflicts between monetary and fiscal policies are re-surfacing. A possible return of fiscal dominance may undermine the autonomy of Central Banks. In the US, for example, the Congress was threatening to put the Federal Reserve System under greater surveillance. Admittedly, the responsibility for financial stability must be shared by both the Government and the Central Bank. Dr Subbarao, Governor, RBI, points out two concerns in this context. First, the rescue of financial institutions is an inherently political act and involvement in such decisions may compromise Central Bank's technocratic credentials. Second, there is the risk that coordination with the government for the purpose of financial stability may spill-over into other areas within the Central Bank's purview thereby undermining its independence. "Central bank independence is perhaps not an unalloyed virtue" and Dr Subba Rao recommends: "Central Banks must advocate for independence not with weighty arguments but through more vigorous and voluntary efforts to be transparent, responsive, and accountable".

As Dr Reddy points out: "First, large sections of the population have[3] been affected by the financial crisis and they consider themselves innocent victims of the crisis in the financial sector. In particular, they feel that those involved in the finance sector have enjoyed disproportionate gains and shifted the pains of adjustment to the rest of the population."[4] Dr Reddy feels that to correct this perception

3. Subbarao (2010).

4. Reddy (2012).

by the majority it is not enough to provide consumer protection and ensure systemic stability.

Imperatives of Inclusive Finance

There is another dimension of the impact of global financial crisis, to which Dr Y.V. Reddy has drawn our attention in his recent Par Jacobson Foundation lecture.[5] The reference here is to erosion of trust in the financial sector as a whole, in particular in banking in the advanced economies. This decline of trust and confidence is partly the result of market failure and relates to incentives—in many cases obscenely high level of remuneration of senior management—and greed. Partly, it is also due to misplaced faith in the self-correcting powers of the market. Whatever may have been the reasons, the resultant effect is clear: "It is evident that public authorities in major financial centres genuinely believed that the financial system, even in its complex evolution, was contributing to the public good. But this fair ex post proved to be misplaced". Dr. Reddy therefore advocates 'inclusive finance'—a commitment to access of essential financial services to all segments of the society. He outlines the course of future action towards achieving this objective.

Society expects Central Banks to restore this trust and confidence in money and finance and move the system towards inclusive finance.

> Society has put its trust in Central Banks. Central Banks have to ensure that bank managements and finance sector in general serve the masses, and not merely the elite or the financially active. In the ultimate analysis, Central Banks are trustees, agents to look after the interest of the masses.

The Indian Experiment

Viewed in this broader context, Indian empirical experience is interesting. The evolution of the Indian financial system is unique in a number of ways. The founding fathers of RBI built into the statute of the RBI the responsibility of promoting agricultural credit. This was rather unusual for a country which was still a British colony. Nationalisation of major commercial banks in 1969, the phenomenal

5. Ibid.

branch expansion programme, unprecedented in the history of world banking and fixing credit targets with a view to ensuring wider disbursal of credit—these were indeed bold steps at that point of time in financial history. Reaching the small borrowers and the poor thus became the objective of the whole financial system. The Indian financial system is thus a product of state and Central Banks direction and guidance. This approach brought about a structural transformation in the deployment of bank credit. The share of large and medium industries in the total credit which was around 61 per cent in March 1968 declined significantly to 38 per cent in June 1982. Simultaneously, the share of priority sectors which include agriculture and small industries rose from 11 per cent to 36 per cent during the period. Those who came to scoff at the Indian experiment have remained to pray.

As a postscript it may be added that more recently top regulators in the US have begun to articulate what needs to be done for banking. Banks have become too complex to manage as opposed to just too big to manage. The biggest banks must become simpler. More broadly, we have lost sight of what banking is supposed to do. Their role is not to assume a huge amount of risk with downside losses covered by society. Wilber Ross the legendary investor states: "I think that the real purpose and the real need that we have in this country for banks is to make loans particularly to small business and to individuals. I think that's the hard part to fill."[6] Back to the basics!

References

Johnson, Simon (2012). "Big Banks: Too Big to Handle", *Economic Times*, October 26.

Prasad, Easwar (2010). "After the Fall", *Finance and Development* 47(2).

Reddy, Y.V. (2012). "Society, Economic Policies and the Financial Sector", *Economic and Political Weekly* XLVIII (33). August 18.

Sharma, Anand (2012). "Financial Stability: 2007 to 2012—Five Years On", *RBI Monthly Bulletin*, October.

Subbarao, Duvuuri (2010). "Redefining Central Banking", *Finance and Development* 47(2): 26-27.

6. Johnson (2012).